KU-537-823

CARD GAMES FOR TWO

David Parlett was born in London in 1939 and brought up in Barry in Wales. He graduated in Modern Languages from the University College of Wales, Aberystwyth, and trained as a teacher.

He has been interested in playing and inventing games since childhood. He is now a consulting editor to *Games & Puzzles* magazine, with which he has been connected since its first appearance in 1972. Since 1974 he has been contributing a monthly column, 'On the Cards', to the magazine and has written numerous other articles and reviews.

David Parlett is also a game inventor. His first published game was 'Hare and Tortoise' and he has followed this with others, of which the card game 'Ninety Nine' is probably the best known. The latter can be found in his book *Card Games for Three*, which is also in the Teach Yourself series.

The author is married and lives in South London.

TEACH YOURSELF BOOKS

For
BARBARA

a game of cards is a labour of love

CARD GAMES FOR TWO

David Parlett

TEACH YOURSELF BOOKS
Hodder and Stoughton

First impression 1978
Third impression 1981

Copyright © 1978
David Parlett

All rights reserved. No part of this publication may be reproduced or transmitted in any form or by any means, electronic or mechanical, including photocopy, recording, or any information storage and retrieval system, without permission in writing from the publisher.

ISBN 0 340 23485 7

Printed and bound in Great Britain for
Hodder and Stoughton Paperbacks,
a division of Hodder and Stoughton Ltd,
Mill Road, Dunton Green, Sevenoaks, Kent
(Editorial Office: 47 Bedford Square, London WC1B 3DP),
by Richard Clay (The Chaucer Press) Ltd,
Bungay, Suffolk

Published in the U.S.A. by David McKay & Co, Inc.,
750 Third Avenue, New York, N.Y. 10017, U.S.A.

CONTENTS

INTRODUCTION

There are more indoor games for two players than for any other number, and cards are no exception. Perhaps the reason is not so hard to find. Two may be company and three a crowd, but there comes a time when you need to stop holding hands and put your brain back into gear.

There are so many good card games for two that I have had no difficulty in choosing what to put in. I might have found it harder to decide what to leave out, but have solved that problem easily enough by omitting (a) two-hand adaptations of games more suited to other numbers of players, such as Bridge, Canasta and so on, and (b) games closely related to but less well known than those already covered; for this reason there is no need for a Rummy game other than Gin, or for Russian Bank as well as Spite and Malice. I have, however, expanded some chapters by including variants on the main subject. That on Bézique, for example, deals with versions played with different numbers of packs, as well as Fildinski or Polish Bézique, which is virtually a different game.

This approach has enabled me to offer a certain amount of variety. Different players prefer different types of game, and I have tried to cater for all tastes without (I hope) too obviously revealing my own preferences and personal dislikes. It may help the process of selection to note that the present contents have fallen so naturally into three groups that I have formally divided the book into three parts to match.

Part I contains English and American games played with a full pack of 52 cards. For the most part they are highly individualistic in character, but quite easy to learn and to play without requiring a painful amount of intellectual endeavour. Many may be recommended for children and beginners.

Part II presents European games played with a short pack of 32 or fewer cards. These are all trick-taking games (see p xi), and give maximum opportunity for the development and application of the highest card skills. Many of them may be recommended for frustrated Bridge players unable to find a third, let alone a fourth player. I must point out that Piquet and Bézique, though now rarely heard of, were among the most popular card games in England until well after the First World War, and deserve to be revived.

Part III gathers together a motley crew of unusual card games whose common factor is that both players start with exactly equal opportunities, and, for the most part, know which cards are held by the other or are otherwise available to him. Such games in some ways contradict the essence of traditional card games, and may well appeal to Chess players and others who prefer games that are, literally, open and above board. This does not mean that they demand more skill than traditional card games; they merely call for thinking of a different type. Nor are they necessarily cerebral. Gops, for example, is pure fun and quite incalculable, while Poker Squares always has been a popular game in the family circle.

My account of each game follows a regular format. First, an introduction to what the game is about, where it comes from and how old it is. This is followed by a straightforward description of how to play the basic game. In this connection it should be noted that few card games are equipped with inviolably authoritative rules of play, and that accounts of the same game by different writers may be expected to reflect the various ways in which it has been played by different people in different places and at different times. I maintain that in card-play, unlike Chess, rules are not made to be obeyed – they are made to obey the tastes and preferences of the players. The only important requirement is that the players should agree in advance on what their particular rules are going to be.

After that may come notes on good play, an illustrative deal or game, and a brief description of variants or closely related games. Whether or not all three of these items appear, and in what order, depends on the game concerned and the dictates of space.

I should like to add a personal note of gratification at having been asked to prepare *Card Games for Two*, which extends and replaces material first presented under that title by the late Kenneth Konstam some twenty five years ago. Not merely because it was Konstam's book which led me into the delights of card play (I had previously preferred Chess), but because the book was bought and the conversion made while my wife and I were on honeymoon. Since we spent much of that time – I have not calculated precisely how much – playing Piquet, and have since progressed to Spite and Malice with equal pleasure, the dedication of this opus goes almost without saying.

NOTE TO THE TEXT

Technical terms are explained on page 165, but note here that 'elder' refers to the non-dealer and 'younger' to the player who dealt. The abbreviation 'T' stands for the Ten-card of any suit. Where appropriate, the winning of a trick is denoted by printing the winning card in italic type eg ◇*A*.

Dealing

The usual way of deciding which player should deal first is for each to draw a card from the pack spread face down on the table. The one drawing the higher card either deals first or has the choice as to whether or not to deal first. The dealer should shuffle the cards thoroughly and, before dealing them out, offer the pack face down for his opponent to cut. The cut is made by lifting off the top half of the pack, putting it to one side, then placing the other half on top of it. A 'half', for this purpose, should contain at least one tenth of the cards in the pack.

Tricks

Many games involve the playing of cards in 'tricks'. The meaning of a 'trick' is as follows. One person plays one of his cards face up to the table, thereby *leading* a card. The other must then (if the rules so require), play one of his own cards belonging to the same suit as the card which was led. Whoever played the card of higher rank wins the trick, which consists of both cards together, and lays it face down on the table before him. The winner then leads to the next trick.

If the second player has no card of the suit led, he may play any card but cannot then win the trick – unless, however, one suit has previously been chosen as the *trump* suit. In this case he can beat any non-trump lead by playing any card of the trump suit, which wins regardless of its rank.

Unless the rules dictate otherwise, the ranks of each suit are, from highest to lowest: A K Q J T 9 8 7 6 5 4 3 2. The suits are generally referred to in the text by their sign; *ie* Spades, ♠; Hearts, ♡; Clubs, ♣; Diamonds, ◇.

PART I
GAMES WITH A FULL PACK

All games of English origin are played with a full pack of 52 cards, consisting of A K Q J T 9 8 7 6 5 4 3 2 in each suit and usually ranking from high to low in that order. Games in this section are varied in character. All Fours is the only one involving tricks. Cribbage, an old English pub game, and Cassino, an Italianate-American game much played by children, involve matching cards together with particular reference to the addition of numbers on their faces. Gin is a collection game, like all forms of Rummy, and Spite and Malice a sort of two-player competitive patience.

I CRIBBAGE

An old English game, said to have been invented in the early 16th century by Sir John Suckling, Cribbage remains popular in all those parts of the world that used to belong to the British Empire, including the American colonies. Suckling's exact contribution to the game is not clear, but he may have added some refinements to an earlier game called Noddy. In passing, it might be mentioned that a somewhat simpler version was described under the name Costly Colours in Charles Cotton's *Compleat Gamester* of 1674.

Cribbage remains essentially a pub game in England, and a rural one at that. One of its chief delights is the necessity of recording scores on a traditional piece of equipment called the crib (or noddy) board, whereby pegs are moved in holes drilled into a block of wood in a distinctive pattern. When both players have the same score they are said to be at 'level pegging', and the game ends when one of them has 'pegged out'. The equipment is needed because points are accumulated and recorded in dribs and drabs continuously throughout the game: it is not a question of waiting until you have finished play and then calculating the rewards for what you have succeeded in doing, which is the way of most other card games.

The original form of Cribbage is played by two players with five cards each, but a six-card game has grown up for two players as well, and is now preferred to the five-card game by most Crib players, except stubborn old die-hards like me.

Beginners, of course, should start with the simpler five-card game and work upwards, and that is the order in which we shall introduce the game and its variants.

Five-card Cribbage

Equipment. A standard 52-card pack, a cribbage board, and four pegs or matchsticks to move around it. (See captioned illustration for method of use.) The crib board is slightly more of a necessity than a convenience, and any form of mechanical scorer that may be available is better than pencil and paper.

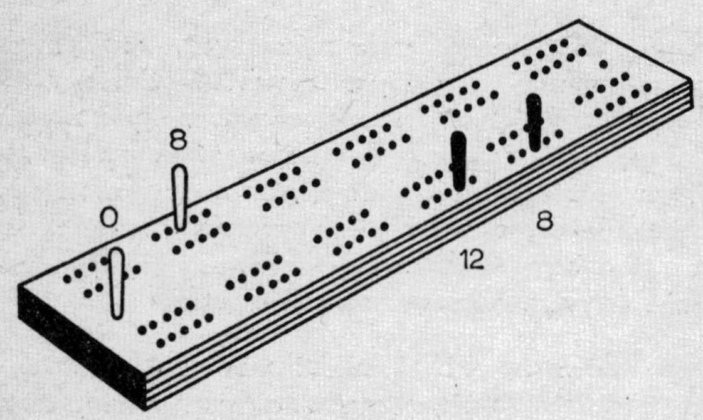

FIGURE I

A 61-hole Cribbage board. Each player starts with one peg in the centre hole (counting 0 or 61) at either end, and one peg in hand. Scores are pegged up the outside and down the inside of each player's double row of holes by moving pegs alternately. Here, white pegs eight on his first deal and indicates that figure by placing his second peg in the eighth hole from the start. Black also pegged eight on his first deal, and has subsequently pegged four, indicated by moving the previously backward peg four holes in front of the other. By this system each player's total score is indicated by his leading peg, his most recent score by the difference between it and his trailing peg. Mistakes in counting are therefore easy to note and to correct. There are also 121- and 181-hole boards, but it is just as convenient to count twice or three times round the 61 board. Additional central holes are sometimes provided for recording games or circuits of the board.

Game. The winner is the first player to attain 61 points, which will take several deals. It may be agreed that if the loser fails to reach 31, he is lurched (or, in the lurch) and loses double. Alternatively, the game may be played up to 121, in which case the lurch is 91.

Deal. Whoever cuts the higher (Ace low) deals first, and his opponent immediately pegs (scores) 'three for last', which is meant to compensate him for the disadvantage of not having the first crib. Subsequently, the turn to deal alternates, but three for last is not scored again in the same game. Deal five cards to each player, one at a time, and place the remainder face down on the table.

Discarding. Each player now looks at his cards, discarding two; the four discards are laid aside face down to form the 'crib'. The crib belongs to the dealer. He may not look at it yet, but at the end of the game any scoring combinations it contains count in his favour. Meanwhile, any scoring combinations formed by the three cards left in each hand will count in favour of their holder. Before discarding, therefore, it is necessary to know what scoring combinations are to be made at Cribbage.

Scoring combinations. The order of cards in each suit is A 2 3 4 5 6 7 8 9 T J Q K. Each card has a point value equivalent to the number of pips on its face, *ie* Ace 1, Two 2, and so on. For this purpose court cards count 10 each, and it is convenient to refer to all cards worth 10 (T J Q K) as 'tenths'. The scoring combinations and the amounts they score are as follows:

Fifteen (any two or more cards totalling exactly 15)	= 2
Pair (two cards of the same rank)	= 2
Prial (= pair royal) (three cards of the same rank)	= 6
Double pair royal (four of the same rank)	= 12
Run (three or more cards in sequence)	= 1 per card
Flush (three cards of one suit in the hand)	= 3
Flush (as above, and start card also of that suit)	= 4
Flush (four crib cards and start card of same suit)	= 5

Some examples of a fifteen are 7–8, 5–Q and A–4–9. A crib containing A–4–4–9 would count fifteen twice: once for A–9 plus the first Four, and again for A–9 plus the second Four; –

the hand would also score 2 for the pair. But a hand of 7–4–4 counts fifteen only once, because the two Fours must be used once together instead of once each in order to make up the total. They still count 2 for the pair, of course.

A pair only counts if both cards are of exactly the same rank, such as Q–Q. Two different tenths, such as J–K, do not pair. A prial scores 6 because it is made up of three different pairs. For example, ♠7–♡7–♣7 counts as (♠7–♡7)+(♡7–♣7)+(♠7–♣7). A double pair royal counts 12 by the same system.

A run is three or more cards in sequence, regardless of suit, such as A–2–3 or 9–T–J–Q. The score is 1 per card in the sequence, *ie* at least 3.

If a player's three hand-cards are of the same suit, he may peg 3 for the flush, or 4 if the start card (see below) also matches. If all four cards of the crib are of the same suit, the crib-holder may count the flush *only* if the start is also of that suit, for a total of 5.

A fundamental principle of Cribbage combinations is that a score is credited for each different combination of cards that can be made, and any individual card may be used in different combinations or more than one of the same type. Thus a hand such as 7–7–8–9 is scored cumulatively as follows: 'Fifteen 2, fifteen 4, pair 6 and two runs of three 12'. Note that the Sevens not only count together as a pair, but also can each be used in turn to score two different fifteens and two different three-card runs.

Let us now return to the game. In discarding to the crib, the dealer will naturally seek to throw cards that tend to combine, whereas his opponent will throw cards that bear no relation to each other. At the same time, both will endeavour to retain cards which go together.

The start. After the discarding, non-dealer cuts the pack and dealer takes the top card of the bottom half and lays it face up on the top. This card is known as the start. If it is a Jack, dealer immediately pegs 'two for his heels'.

The play. Before any combinations are scored, the cards are played as follows. Starting with non-dealer, each in turn plays one of his cards face up to the table in front of himself. (The two players' cards must not get mixed up.) Non-dealer announces the face value of his first card, and as each subsequent card appears its player announces the cumulative total of all cards so far played. Thus if the first cards are Four, Nine, Two, the announcements are 'four–thirteen–fifteen' and so on. If either player adds a card which forms a scoring combination when considered in conjunction with the previous card or cards consecutively played, he is entitled to announce and peg for it. For example: Non-dealer 'Four'; dealer (playing a Six) 'Ten'; non-dealer (playing a Five): 'Fifteen 2 and a run of three, 5'. That is, he scores 2 for bringing the count to fifteen, and 3 for forming the three-card sequence 4–5–6, even though they did not actually appear in that order. If now dealer adds a Three, he announces 'Eighteen and a run (of four) 4', as he has thereby extended the sequence into one of 3–4–5–6. Pairs, prials and double pairs royal may be made and pegged in the same way, so long as the cards they combine with were played consecutively, *ie* without interruption by an extraneous card not belonging to the combination. Thus if the first four cards were 6–7–5–5, the first Five would make a run of three and the second would make a pair, but the second would not make a run of three as it has been separated from the Six and Seven by another card. Again, 6–7–4 scores nothing, but if the next card played were a Five it would make a four-card sequence for 4 points. In the play, flushes do not count.

31 and go. The play continues so long as neither player brings the combined count above 31. If a player cannot add a card without exceeding this total, he must pass by announcing 'go', whereupon the other must add as many more cards as he can without exceeding 31. Whoever plays the last card pegs 'one for last', or 'two' if he brings the count to exactly 31.

Counting the hand. Each player now retrieves his cards and scores for any combinations they contain, non-dealer doing so first. For this purpose each player considers the start (turned-up card) as if it formed part of his own hand. For example, if the start were a Six, a player holding 4–5–6 would score 12 altogether. If the three cards of his hand are all of the same suit, he counts 3 for the flush, and if the start is also of that suit, he counts 4 instead. Furthermore, whoever holds the Jack of the same suit as the start pegs 'one for his nob'. After non-dealer has counted his hand, dealer counts his own on exactly the same basis. Finally, dealer turns up the cards of the crib and scores this as if it were yet another hand. Again, the start is counted as part of it, making it a five-card hand altogether, and the Jack of the turned suit scores one for his nob. The only difference is a restriction on flushes: a flush only counts if all five cards are of the same suit – it is not enough for the four discards to be alike in suit if the start is different.

Muggins (*optional*). An optional but recommended rule is that if either player omits to score anything to which he is entitled, his opponent may draw attention to it (with a cry of 'muggins') and score it himself.

Ending. As soon as one player reaches the target score, play ceases at whatever stage it has reached. This may be as the result of turning a Jack for start, or playing to the count, or counting either of the hands or the crib, or scoring by the rule of muggins, or by means of a penalty.

Penalties. A 2-point penalty (added to the aggrieved party's score) is counted for each of the following irregularities: (1) In the deal, exposing one of non-dealer's cards, or dealing him too many; in the former case he may demand a redeal, and in the latter a redeal is compulsory. (2) For touching the undealt pack except to cut and turn the start. (3) During the play, for failing to add a card although able to do so without exceeding 31. Furthermore, if it is discovered that a player has pegged more than his entitlement, he must reduce his score to the correct amount, and the amount by which he overpegged is credited to his opponent.

Six-card Cribbage

(This account assumes knowledge of the five-card game, anything unexplained being the same as described above.)

Game. Game may be set as 121, with (optionally) 91 for the lurch and 61 for the double lurch, or at 181, with 121 for the lurch.

Deal. After cutting for first deal, there is no scoring of three for last. Deal six cards each one at a time.

Discard. Each player discards two cards to a crib, which belongs to the dealer.

Start. Non-dealer cuts and dealer turns up the start, counting 2 for his heels if it is a Jack. (This score seems to be increasingly ignored by modern players.)

Play. Non-dealer leads and cards are played up to 31 as at the five-card game, with scores for fifteen, pairs, runs, 'go' and making 31. If, however, either player has cards left unplayed from hand, those so far played are turned face down and a new series is played with the remaining cards up to (but not over) 31 as before, the first card being led by the opponent of the player who played the last of the previous series. If this still fails to exhaust all the cards, yet a third series is started.

Counting the hand. As before, non-dealer then counts the start as part of his hand and scores for all the combinations he can make from the five cards. Then dealer does the same, and finally counts his crib, consisting of four cards and the start. A flush consists of four cards in hand for 4, plus a fifth if the start is of the same suit. A flush in the crib scores only if the start matches, for 5.

Seven-card Cribbage

As six-card, except that game is 181 and seven cards are dealt to each player. Each discards two to the crib and counts a six-card hand including the start. This form of the game is little played.

Auction Cribbage

This variant, which I suspect to have been invented by the late Hubert Phillips, injects an additional element of judgement and may be commended for that reason, though I have never met anyone who plays it. The principle may be applied to the game whether played with five, six or seven cards, and the idea is that the crib does not necessarily belong to the dealer but may be won by bidding for it. After dealing, the dealer states how many points he is prepared to pay for the privilege of the crib; non-dealer may raise this amount, dealer re-raise it and so on until one of them passes. The other then immediately deducts from his score the amount he is prepared to pay, and play proceeds. The start is turned, both discard as usual, and the opponent of the crib-holder leads the first card and also counts his hand first after the play. Phillips, the only source I know for the game (in *The Pan Book of Card Games*), does not state what happens if neither is prepared to bid. I suggest that if both pass the start should be turned and each have another opportunity to bid. If both still pass, which is unlikely, the hands are thrown in and the next in turn deals.

Square Cribbage

This variation was devised by me and is also intended to increase the skill factor. It may be played auction-wise as described above, but is essentially a six-card game.

1. Deal six cards each and discard two to the crib in the usual way. Do not yet turn a card for start.
2. Starting with non-dealer, or whoever does not have the crib, each in turn scores for any combinations he may hold on his own four cards. Anything he scores for must be shown, but it is not obligatory to declare everything one has.
3. Now the start card is turned in the usual way, dealer scoring 2 for his heels if it is a Jack. The start is placed face up in the middle of the table.
4. Starting with the opponent of the crib-holder, each in turn

plays a card to the table in such a way as to gradually build up a square of $3 \times 3 = 9$ cards, with the start card in the centre. There is no counting up to 31.

5. A player scores for any combination he makes between the card he plays and any other card or cards in the same row, column or long diagonal, as at noughts and crosses (eight directions in all). A three-card flush is valid, but it is impossible to make a four-card run or double pair royal. Combinations may be scored in more than one direction simultaneously, provided that each one involves the card just played. For playing the Jack of the same suit as the centre card (the start), score one for his nob.
6. When all eight cards have been played, the crib-holder turns the crib and counts it in the usual way, including the start (centre card of the square) as part of it. A flush must contain five cards as usual.

The point of this variation is that each player enters it with some knowledge of his opponent's cards, *ie* of those scored at the beginning, and will therefore be guided by this knowledge in his planning of where and when to place cards in the square. Higher scores are made because any given card may be scored in up to three directions at once.

Notes on play (basic 5- and 6-card)

Cribbage has been noted as one of the few games in which memory does not play an important part. At the same time, it is one of the foremost of those in which experience leads rapidly to intuitive and unerringly correct play. The well-practised player does not need to think overmuch about the discard or play of a given hand – similar situations will have come up so often before that he will know by looking at his cards the best course of action to take. The beginner, however, must go slowly at first, and will have to consider several alternatives before making a decision. It is to this end that the following notes may be of help. They are written from the viewpoint of the five-card game, but much the same principles apply to six-card, which is the same thing only bigger.

First, it is important to realise that Cribbage is scored, as I have remarked before, in dribs and drabs – two points here, two points there, one for his nob, and so on. For this reason a fundamental law of the game is that *every point counts*. Look after the pennies, as they say, and the pounds will take care of themselves. Even when deciding which cards to throw to the crib, you must take into account whether or not the cards remaining might enable you, with correct play, to score a go in the play up to 31. There is only one point in it, but it might be vital. The highest possible score in the crib is 29, but an average value is 4, and quite a few are complete duds. In Cribbage you must fight for odd points. Don't sit back and expect them to come out in the wash.

Your first strategic decision in the game is what to throw to the crib. If the crib is yours, throw cards that combine well, such as a Five and a tenth, a pair, or at the very least two cards in sequence, as there is a good chance of improving any of these with the aid of the cards thrown by your opponent plus the start. A Five and a tenth, scoring 'fifteen 2', make a good discard, as the chances are roughly 4 in 13 that the start will be a tenth, while it is often difficult for the non-dealer to avoid throwing a tenth to the crib.

If the crib is not yours, throw cards unlikely to combine well, and certainly not combinable with each other. You cannot guard much against the likelihood that one of your cards will pair with the start or one of the other discards, but you can fight sequences by throwing cards widely separated in rank. From the viewpoint of fifteens it is clearly essential not to throw a Five, as there are too many chances of there being tenths in the crib. There is somewhat less danger involved in throwing a tenth, as the chances are much against your opponent's holding a Five (especially if you have one yourself), or the appearance of one as the start. But keep back a tenth if you can discard anything safer, and always keep back a Jack on the principle of counting the pennies – you may score one for his nob. You must, of course, ensure that the two cards you throw do not total five or fifteen, and ten is to be avoided if possible. There is always also the danger that a start lower than Five will combine to total five with another low card in the crib.

Neither player should bother about a flush in the crib. If the crib is yours you are unlikely to get one, and if it is your opponent's you need not spoil your hand to avoid throwing two of a suit. A flush in the hand is only worth holding as compensation for lack of combining possibilities, and is not worth keeping back at the expense of good cards for the play.

The other side of the discarding coin is consideration of which cards to keep in hand – not only for the combinations they may score between them, but also for the play. In the latter connection it is generally preferable to keep low cards. So, all things being equal, prefer to throw high cards to the crib.

Choice of discards may also be modified by the state of the score. If you have the crib when both are within reach of game, do not waste good cards on a high-scoring crib. Remember that the crib is counted last, and your opponent may peg out before you get a chance to use it. In this case retain cards more likely to score at the earliest opportunity – in the play.

In the play, the best cards to lead from a numerical viewpoint are those lower than Five, as they cannot be fifteened with one card (from which point of view, the worst possible lead is a Five). The best lead is a Four; lower ranks are more usefully retained to score a go as 31 is reached.

From the viewpoint of the structure of your hand, a good lead is one of a pair, in the hope that your opponent will pair it and give you a prial, as the danger of his then making a double pair royal is pretty remote. It is also reasonable to lead cards close in rank, with a view to making a sequence, especially if there is the chance of your making a run of four without his gaining an intervening three.

Playing second and given the choice, prefer to make the lead up to fifteen than to pair the first card, in case it was led from a pair in the hope of a prial. Generally, if your own cards are close in rank you may 'play on' – that is, play ranks close to those of your opponent with a view to making runs. If they are widely separated, it is better to 'play off' by always seeking to play a card remote in rank from the previous one.

Once past the half-way mark, always avoid bringing the count to 21, as there are too many cards in the pack to make it 31 next. It is also important to avoid halving the total needed to make 31 exactly, as your opponent may then score 4 for the pair and the 31. (For example, at 23, which is eight short, don't play a Four. That makes 27, and another Four scores high.)

Finally, keep careful track of both players' positions. When leading, don't mind giving your opponent 2 for a fifteen if you can then pair it for 2 yourself, as he will not gain on you and you will be closer to home. When trailing, however, take every reasonable chance to reduce the difference, and if this is not possible then prefer that neither should score rather than both; e.g., don't pair the lead if you think he can make it 15.

Illustrative deals

Two deals from a game at Five-card Cribbage should show how the game goes and what sort of decisions must be made. Our players are Alf and Bert; the former cuts a King and is 'in the box' first, dealing:

First deal

A: ♡2 ♠5 ♢8 ♣T ♡T
B: ♡3 ♢7 ♣7 ♣8 ♢9

Alf seems to have an embarrassment of riches – three fifteens and a pair, something of which will have to be broken up. If he keeps ♠5 ♣T ♡T, worth 6, he must throw to the crib ♡2 ♢8, which is unlikely to make anything as a Five discarded or turned up is too remote to think of. As there is more chance of a tenth, he discards ♠5 ♣T to his crib and retains ♡2 ♢8 ♡T for the play.

Bert's hand is hardly less prolific, containing a pair, two fifteens and a couple of runs to boot. But ♡3 and ♢9 would make good discards (provided that there is no other Three in the crib), so he breaks the runs and keeps ♢7 ♣7 ♣8.

The ♠A is turned as the start, and Bert leads:

B: ♢7 (= 7)
A: ♢8 (= 15) pegs fifteen–2
B: ♣8 (= 23) pegs pair 2
A: ♡2 (= 25)
B: 'go'
A: pegs 1 for last, as he cannot play further.

Now Bert counts his hand: fifteen 2, fifteen 4, fifteen 6 (counting the start to make ♠A ♢7 ♣7), and a pair 8, plus 2 in play 10.

Alf counts his: nothing in hand, 3 in play. And the crib: fifteen–2, fifteen–4. Total 7. A poor result. Had he discarded his pair of Tens and retained ♡2 ♠5 ♢8 he would have finished with an extra point. In principle, however, the discard of ♠5 ♣T should have met at least another tenth for an extra 2.

Second deal. Bert deals

B: ♠3 ♣6 ♠Q ♠K ♢K
A: ♢2 ♢4 ♠4 ♣J ♡K

Bert's problem is whether to keep the flush for 3, discarding ♣6 ♢K to his own crib, or the pair of Kings intact in hand or crib. If the latter, should he retain ♠Q ♠K ♢K in the hope of turning a Jack for two runs, throwing ♠3 ♣6, or throw the two Kings and keep ♠3 ♣6 ♠Q as being good cards for the play? He chooses the last possibility, discarding both Kings.

Alf has no such problem: he will keep the pair and the Jack, discarding ♢2 ♡K, fairly innocuous-looking cards for his opponent's crib.

The start is ♣5, and play proceeds:

A: ♢4 (= 4)
B: ♠3 (= 7)

A: ♣J (= 17)
B: ♣6 (= 23)
A: ♠4 (= 27)
B: 'go'
A: 1 for last.

Bert hesitated before playing his Six. Bringing the count to 23 gave Alf more scope than bringing it to 27 would have done, but the former has already shown a Four and a Jack. Since Alf must have kept his best cards for the hand, he may well have another Four, which would give him an extra hole for making 31.

Alf now counts his hand (◇4 ♠4 ♣J and the start ♣5): fifteen–2, pair 4, one for his nob 5, plus 1 for last 6.

Bert's is ♠3 ♣6 ♠Q and start ♣5, worth fifteen–2 only. His crib, however, brings a rich haul: ◇2 ♡K ◇K ♠K and the start ♣5 counts fifteen–2, fifteen–4, fifteen–6, prial 12, total 15 to Alf's 6.

2 GIN RUMMY

Gin is the simplest, the earliest and probably the best of the large family of Rummy games, which all work on the same principles and differ from one another only in degrees of complication. Though it reached its hey-day during the 30s–40s golden age of Hollywood ('the game of the stars'), it seems first to have been described in more or less its present form during the first decade of the present century. It bears striking similarities to the southern-states negro game of Coon Can, which lies in direct line of descent from the first recorded Rummy game, Con Quian, played in Mexico in the middle of the last century. The whole family has always been particularly associated with Latin America, as witnessed by such later elaborations as Canasta (the word is Spanish and the place of origin Uruguay) and its derivatives Bolivia, Samba and so on.

The object in Rummy games is to collect cards which 'go together', either being of the same rank, like ♠7 ♡7 ♣7, or forming a sequence in the same suit, such as ♠7 ♠8 ♠9. Such a matching collection is called a *meld*. Any cards left in one's hand at the end of a deal which fail to form a meld of three or more are called *deadwood*, and incur penalties equivalent to their combined face values. The method by which cards are collected for this purpose will probably be well known even to non card-players. At each turn you draw a card from a stockpile and throw out an unwanted card to a discard pile, and keep doing so until all the cards you hold can be arranged in matching sets, or melds. It is a method which is to be found in essence in the game of Mah Jong, and which has been borrowed as part of the mechanics of many modern table games. One could even claim to recognise it in Monopoly, by noting that you may not build upon a property until you have formed it into part of a 'meld' of three properties of the same colour.

Gin Rummy is very easy to learn and the rules are clear, simple, and fairly well standardised.

The game

Cards. One standard 52-card pack; no Jokers.

Game. The game is won by the first player to reach 100 points, which normally takes several deals.

Rank and value of cards. Cards rank A 2 3 4 5 6 7 8 9 T J Q K and are worth their face value, with Ace 1 and court cards 10 each.

Deal. Whoever cuts the higher card chooses whether or not to deal first. Thereafter the winner of one hand deals to the next, and the winner of a game deals first to the next. It is important that the cards be thoroughly shuffled before play, dealer having the right to shuffle last. Deal ten cards each, one at a time. Place the remainder face down to form a stock. Take the top card of the stock and lay it face up beside it to form the first 'upcard'. This will form the base of a gradually constituted waste pile of faced cards, the topmost of which is always known as the upcard.

To start. Nondealer may start by exchanging the upcard for any card in his hand. If he refuses, dealer has the same privilege. If either player does so, that constitutes his first turn and the game continues from there. If both refuse it, nondealer must start the game by drawing the top card of the stock, adding it to his hand, and discarding any card face up on the original upcard to continue the waste pile.

Play. Thereafter, each player in turn must draw and add to his hand either the unknown top card of the stock, or the faced upcard surmounting the waste pile. In either case he completes his turn by making one discard face up to the waste pile. It is not permissible to draw the upcard and discard it on the same turn.

Object. The object is to collect cards which together form one or more melds, a meld consisting of either (a) three or four cards of the same rank, or (b) a sequence of three or more cards in the same suit, such as ♠A 2 3 . . . or . . . ♡T J Q K. (For this purpose, Ace and King are not consecutive.) A hand consisting entirely of melds, with no deadwood, is described as 'gin' and carries a bonus. But a player may end the game as soon as the total value of his unmatched cards is 10 or less, at which point the player with the lower value of deadwood wins. During play, melds are not revealed but retained secretly in the hand.

Knocking. When a player is satisfied with the low value of his deadwood, he ends the game by (theoretically) knocking on the table after he has drawn an eleventh card and before making his final discard. It is now the practice to indicate closure of the game by laying the final discard face down on the waste pile, an action still referred to as knocking. The knocker then spreads his hand of cards face up on the table, arranged in melds and with any deadwood clearly separated from them. His opponent then does the same, but also has the privilege of 'laying off' any cards of his own deadwood which may be matched with any of the knocker's melds, in order to reduce the penalty value of his deadwood. This privilege does not apply, however, if the knocker has a gin hand (no deadwood).

End of stock. The two last cards of the stock may not be taken. If neither player has knocked by the time they are reached, the result is a no-score draw, and the same dealer deals again.

Score. Each player keeps his score cumulatively, the winner of a hand adding his score for the hand to his previous total and writing down the combined amount in order to make clear when 100 has been reached or exceeded.

If the knocker has the lower count for deadwood, he scores the difference between the two deadwood values. If he went gin, he adds a bonus of 25.

If the opponent has an equal or lower value of deadwood, he scores the difference (if any) plus a bonus of 25 for undercut. But he cannot undercut a gin hand, for which the knocker still counts 25, nor may he himself score the bonus for gin, whether he had it already (in which case he should have knocked) or acquired it by laying off.

Game score. As soon as either player has reached or exceeded 100 points, the game ends and a line is drawn beneath both totals, beneath which various bonuses are recorded. First, the winner records a bonus of 100 for game; next, he adds a 25-point 'box' bonus for each hand that he won. Finally, if he won every hand he adds a bonus for 'shut-out'. This is equivalent to twice the basic amount he scored plus another 100 for game. (In some circles, the box bonuses are also doubled. Other bonus systems may be encountered, but the one described here is usual American practice.) The difference between the two final totals is the margin of victory.

Hollywood scoring system. For those who can't get enough of it, this is a method of playing three games simultaneously (or more if preferred, following the same principle). Three sets of double columns are drawn up, each double column headed by the initials of the players. When a player wins his first hand, his score is recorded in the first set only. When he wins his second, it is recorded in the first and second sets. His third, and so on, is recorded in all three, unless and until any of them has been ruled off with a win. As soon as a player reaches 100 in any of the three sets of columns, that set is ruled off and bonuses noted in the usual way. Play continues until all games have been completed and scored.

Oklahoma variant. In this version the maximum count of deadwood with which you may knock is not necessarily 10, but is determined by the value of the initial upcard. For instance, if it is a Six you must have six or less to knock; if a King, ten. It is usually agreed that if the first upcard is an Ace, you must have a gin hand to go out. The variant may be recommended for the variety it adds to the game.

Suggestions for play

Gin is a game of observation, inference and memory, in that order. Each player's management of his own hand is a somewhat mechanical affair in the sense that for any given situation there is a fairly calculable best move. It is because there is a 'best' move that observation is the foremost aspect of skill required. You *observe* what your opponent is discarding and which of your discards he is drawing; from that, *infer* the structure of his hand on the assumption that he is either making the best moves or acting in accordance with a personal style of play to which you have become accustomed; and thereafter *remember* all the cards that have gone and the changing contents of your opponent's hand as the play proceeded.

As to the play of your own hand, the first thing to note is the inadvisability of going all out for gin. The bonus of 25 is not sufficient to compensate for the times when you should have knocked instead of waiting around for glory, and thereby found yourself more knocked against than knocking. And, worse still, being undercut for your pains. A typical game ends about half to two thirds of the way through the pack, so if you get a knocking hand much earlier than that do not hesitate to go down for all you can get.

It is generally better to draw the stock card than the upcard. The more upcards you draw, the more of your hand is known to the other side, and the more of the rest of it can be deduced. You are also taking cards of no use to your opponent, when by drawing the next card of stock you may well be preventing him from going gin. The best exception to the rule is when you need the upcard to convert two matching cards into a meld of three, thus eliminating three pieces of deadwood (including the discard), or, of course, when it enables you to knock immediately. It may also be useful to expand a meld, especially if you thereby eliminate a high unmatched card; but this should be done with caution rather than as a matter of course, as it can do more harm than good. If, for example, you hold

♠K ♡K ♣K, ◇7 8 9, ♠5, ◇5, ♡2, ♣2

it is not worth taking ◇T as the upcard, as you must then throw one of a pair and so halve the number of draws that will enable you to knock. One other conceivable reason for taking the upcard might be to reduce your deadwood when you suspect an imminent knocking from the other side of the table. The lower the rank he discarded, the worse the danger would appear to be.

Because it is desirable to throw high cards instead of low ones, in order to keep your deadwood down, it is also reasonable to retain high-ranking pairs and two-card sequences acquired early in the game, in the hope that your opponent will discard a matching third in exchange for a lower-valued draw. But this should not be kept up too long. When to give up such expectations and start reducing deadwood is a matter for fine judgement.

Keeping track of discards is fundamental to the play. Suppose your opponent throws ♣J. The easy assumption is that he is 'not collecting Jacks', so you discard ♡J at the next opportunity – and are surprised to see him pounce on it. Too late you spot the ruse. He might have held ♡9 ♡T ♣J and thrown the Jack to draw one of the proper suit for the sequence. Even more cunningly, and perhaps at greater risk (depending on how well he knew the contents of your hand) he might have discarded from ♠J ♢J ♣J. Why, then, should he run a risk to bluff the fourth out of you? Because he thereby not only re-forms his meld, but also prevents you from laying off a Jack when he goes out on the next turn, and perhaps undercutting him.

Of course, what's sauce for the gander is sauce for the goose, and you are at liberty to practise such stratagems yourself. And here's another. Suppose he throws a Jack and you have two Jacks. You are tempted to take it immediately and complete a meld. But resist! He might have been playing from a pair. If so, leave it. He will be bound to throw the other Jack, and then you can take it and be certain that he cannot lay off against that meld of yours and be in a position to undercut. For this to work, you must be pretty sure that he was playing from a pair to start with, and that he is not retaining the other Jack as part of a sequence. If all the Tens and Queens have gone, there is no danger of the latter; and if you have held your Jacks for some time, there is a fair chance that his discard was made from two. If it does go wrong, there is still the chance that either you will draw the other Jack or he will draw and discard it before too great damage is done. Unless he knows every card in your hand, he would be unlikely to draw it and keep it.

So much depends upon observation and remembrance of the contents of the waste pile that you must clearly be very careful in your choice of discard. The first card *not* to throw out is the one you have just drawn from stock and are still holding in your hand: if it really is useless, don't let him know. Hang on to it for a turn or two before getting rid of it. On general principles, as we have seen, it is desirable to throw out a high unmatched card in order to reduce deadwood. The time not to do so is when you suspect that it might be of use to your opponent. In particular, he might be deliberately forcing a card out of you by one of the bluffing stratagems described above, in which case you must hold it back for a turn or two. Check this by matching your proposed discard against the current upcard. The less relation it bears to it, by rank and suit, the better. One player of my acquaintance insists that the ideal discard is different in suit from, but adjacent in rank to, the existing upcard.

It is possible to select a discard in such a way as to elicit useful information. Suppose you have to split up ♠K ♡K, ♠Q ♣Q. In this case throw ♠K. If it is picked up you will know he has the other Kings (in which case you keep yours to lay off if necessary), since your own holding of the Queen shows that he cannot need it for the sequence.

In arranging your melds after knocking, prefer to attach a card to a set of four rather than a sequence if it could equally well go with either. In this way you certainly prevent your opponent from laying off against it, whereas with a sequence there is the danger that he may hold (and therefore lay off) an odd card that attaches to one end of it.

In brief, play your own hand with methodical accuracy, and devote all your thinking to the constitution of the waste pile and the probable structure of your opponent's hand. Above all, remain flexible. Don't select a hoped-for meld at the start of play and concentrate upon it fixedly: circumstances will require you to change plans at a moment's notice.

Illustrative deal

The players are Abe and Blondie, which latter deals as follows:

Abe	♠Q 6 A, ♡T 8, ♣K 8 4, ◇J T,
Blondie	♠T 9, ♡5 A, ♣T 3, ◇7 6 4 2,

The upcard is ♡4, which both players refuse. Abe has several pairs and one two-card sequence, but the rest are unrelated and somewhat high in value. He might have done better to take the upcard and start reducing deadwood by discarding ♠Q. Blondie has a pair of Tens and a promising collection of diamonds. In the account below, the first card shown is the card drawn from stock and the one in brackets represents the discard. UP means the upcard (previous player's discard) is drawn.

A: ♡7 (♠6) Makes a two-card sequence.

B: ♡3 (♡5) Her only discard if the Tens are to be kept.

A: ♡9 (♣K) This makes a four-card sequence including ♡T, which can still be detached and used with ◇T if a black Ten is drawn. The discard reduces deadwood and only runs the risk of being taken if Blondie has a pair of Kings or Queen, Jack of clubs. Kings and Aces are good discards because they do not easily enable the opponent to make sequences.

B: ♣J (♠9) Keeping her pair of Tens, and swapping one two-card sequence for another to avoid throwing out the same card as drawn, which might be observed.

A: ♣Q (♣8) Abe splits his Eights, hoping to draw ♡9 to attach to ♡8 and ♡T (not a commendable expectation), and that Blondie might discard a Queen.

B: ♠3 (♣J) This gives her a meld of Threes and enables her to lose a fairly safe piece of high-counting deadwood, as she holds ♣T while ♣K has already gone.

A: ♣5 (◇T) Abe splits his Tens, as the game is progressing without his having drawn anything useful for high-counting combinations.

B: UP (◇2) Blondie grabs this Ten for another meld – though had she read the previous section she might have left it until he discarded the second in order to prevent him from laying off. She doesn't like discarding such a low card (and Abe is duly dismayed by the sight of it), but must keep ♢7–6.

A: ♡K (♢J) He certainly won't throw the other Ten.

B: ♠J (♠J) By discarding the card drawn, Blondie shows that her hand is now ossified, and that she needs one of several specific cards to knock.

A: ♣A (♡K) A valuable draw, reducing deadwood by nine.

B: ♣7 (♢4) This doubles her chances of knocking, for besides ♢8 and ♢5 there are two Sevens that will make a meld on which to go out.

A: ♣6 (♣Q) Makes a club sequence and reduces deadwood by 19.

B: ♠8 (♠8) A useless card.

A: ♡6 (♠Q face down) Knocks.

Abe's melds are: ♡T–9–8–7–6, ♣6–5–4, leaving ♠A and ♣A for deadwood counting 2 against.

Blondie lays off ♣7 against Abe's club sequence, melds T♠–♣–♢, 3♠–♡–♣, and counts 14 for the remaining deadwood, namely ♢7 ♢6 ♡A. Abe wins, counting towards game Blondie's 14 minus his 2, a score of 12.

Note the strong element of luck in those last two draws. Had Blondie drawn ♠7 instead of ♠8 she would have knocked with deadwood of 1 against Abe's 12, giving her 11 to game. Note, too, that the game ended on the fifteenth out of thirty possible draws – exactly half way through the pack.

3 ALL FOURS

This old English game, of Kentish origin, is the two-player ancestor of the modern American game of Auction Pitch (see *Teach Yourself Card Games for Four*). Along with our native Cribbage, to which it has a curiously similar flavour though being quite different in structure, neither it nor any of its relatives have spread to the rest of Europe. As it is now played little in its country of origin, except sporadically as a pub game in a few unconnected localities, it would probably be regarded as extinct were it not for the fact that its emigration to the colonial Americas gave it a new lease of life on the western side of the Atlantic. For much of the last century, All Fours and its derivatives were among the most popular card games in the United States and Mexico. All Fours itself survives in America under the name Seven Up, which is the form described below, along with such derivatives as California Jack (see page 33), All Fives, Pitch, Cinch, and various games which include the name 'Pedro' in the title.

All Fours may be characterised as a fast little gambling game at which success depends less on cerebral calculation than on long experience. The title of the game is presumed to refer to the four major scoring features of play, namely High, Low, Jack, and the Game.

The game

Cards. A standard 52-card pack.

Game. The winner is the first player to reach a previously agreed total, formerly 11 points in the English game but now 7 in the American – whence the alternative title 'Seven Up'. This will take several deals to achieve. Scores may be recorded on paper, though a traditional method is to start with seven counters each and pay them into a pool one at a time for each point won, so that the winner is the first to get rid of his seven counters.

Deal. Whoever cuts the higher-ranking card deals first; thereafter the turn to deal alternates. Deal a batch of three cards face down to each player, then a second batch of three so that each receives a hand of six cards. Lay the remainder face down to one side, and turn the top card face up.

The turn-up. The suit of the turn-up proposes a trump suit for the deal, which may or may not be accepted by either player. If the turn-up is a Jack, the dealer scores 1 point for it.

Object. The object in each hand is to score as many points as possible, single points being available for one or more of the following factors:

> *Turning a Jack*, as explained above.
> *Gift*, as explained below in the bidding.
> *High*, for having been dealt the highest trump in play.
> *Low*, for having been dealt the lowest trump in play (or, if agreed beforehand, for winning it in a trick).
> *Jack*, for winning a trick containing the Jack of trumps, if it is in play.
> *Game*, for capturing, in tricks, the highest aggregate value of scoring-cards, valued thus: each Ace 4, King 3, Queen 2, Jack 1, Ten 10. In the event of a tie this point goes to elder hand (non-dealer) – this is to offset younger's advantage of scoring a point for turning a Jack.

It is to be noted that the first two points (turning a Jack and Gift) will not always occur, and that there can be no point for winning the Jack if it is not in play, *ie* lies in the undealt part of the pack. Two or more of the points for High, Low and Jack may be combined in one card. For instance, if a given card is the *only* trump in play then it counts one for High plus one for Low. Similarly, the Jack of trumps will count an extra point if it is the highest or the lowest in play. In the extreme case, it would count four if it were the only trump in play (High, Low, Jack) and also the only scoring card in play (giving its winner Game).

Bidding. The bidder is the player who eventually chooses trumps. He is not obliged to reach any particular target and is not penalised for losing, but will naturally select a suit which he thinks will yield him more points than his opponent. Elder hand has first choice: he may accept the turned suit as trump by saying 'I stand', or reject it by saying 'I beg'. If he begs, younger may also accept or reject the proposed trump, but it costs him a point to accept. He accepts by saying 'Take it', in which case elder scores 1 point for Gift and play begins. He rejects the suit by putting the turn-up to one side and 'running the cards', as follows.

Running the cards. To find another suit for trumps, younger first deals another batch of three to each player, so that both have nine cards, and turns up the top card of the pack again. If it is a different suit, the same procedure applies: he scores a point if it is a Jack, then elder may stand or beg, and, if he begs, younger may accept the suit by giving elder a point or reject it by running the cards yet again, dealing three more to each. This continues until either the pack runs out, in which case the hands are thrown in and the cards reshuffled and redealt by the same dealer, or a suit is accepted as trump. Whenever the turn-up proves to be of the same suit as one that has already been rejected, the cards are run again automatically. Younger may not score a point for turning the Jack of a suit that has already been rejected.

Play. If the cards have been run, each player makes as many discards as are necessary to reduce his playing hand to six cards again. Non-dealer leads to the first trick, and the winner of each trick leads to the next. Normal rules of trick-taking apply, but with an important exception – namely, that the second to a trick is always entitled to play a trump, even if he can follow suit. It is not permissible, however, to play from a different non-trump suit if able to follow suit to the card led. A trick is won by the higher card of the suit led or by a higher trump if any are played.

Score. At the end of play each reckons his score for high, low, Jack and game. It is to be noted that points are scored strictly in the order stated, and that as soon as one player has the point which brings his total to seven he has won the game. When played for money, each game is settled separately for a fixed amount.

Notes on play

In all games of this family, custom varies as to whether the point for Low is scored by the player who happens to be dealt the lowest trump in play, or by the player who captures it in a trick – which may, of course, be the same player if he uses it to trump with, but need not always be so. In the original game it went always to the player dealt it. In modern games such as Auction Pitch it goes to the player who captures it, though there is a tendency in two-hand play to revert to the original system. There are those who argue that if the point goes to the player who wins it then credit is given for skill rather than luck. On the other hand, it requires hardly less judgement to decide whether or not your lowest trump – the Four, for example – is in fact likely to be the lowest in play. In short, the only matter of any import is that you should agree beforehand which rule to follow.

The strategy of All Fours depends entirely on the score. At love-all you will be looking for a hand that offers at least two and preferably three of the four potential points, and without losing one for gift for the sake of getting it. At the other extreme, with only one point short of game you can safely entrump any suit of which you hold the Ace, as you will win with the inevitable 'one for High' no matter how many of the others your opponent gains.

You are bound to win the point for High if you hold the Ace of trumps. If the cards have not been run, you can reckon the King as high (and, conversely, the Three as low) about nine times out of ten, and the Queen high (Four low) about four times out of five.

Never bank on the point for Jack unless you have it yourself, and well guarded at that, normally with at least two other trumps.

The point for game is the only one that depends upon the skill with which you play your cards. In this connection, it is essential to save any Ten you hold, as its capture is usually enough to swing the point for Game. For the same reason, it is better, if at all possible, to use Aces and Kings to capture adverse leads than to lead them in their own right. As capturing cards they stand to ensure the point for Game by taking others that may also be of value, whereas, as leaders, they risk being trumped.

A hand containing three or more trumps is usually worth playing – the more so if it includes high ranks or the Jacks, the less so if it lacks these or includes an unguarded Ten. A two-trump hand may be playable if it includes the Ace or King. If you are scoring Low for being dealt it, and have the lead, you may also chance your arm on (say) Q–2 by leading the Two and hoping to force out a singleton Ace or King. If it works, you may gain Game and Low against your opponent's High only.

Related games

All Fives. This increases the number of points to be played for. Game is usually set at 61 and progress recorded on a Cribbage board. In addition to the single points for High, Low, Jack and Game, the following trumps score as below to the player capturing them in tricks:

Ace	4
King	3
Queen	2
Jack	1
Ten	10
Five	5

This gives a maximum of 29 points obtainable on one deal if all the value cards are in play. (In counting for 'Game', the Five of trumps is also worth five, but plain suit Fives have no value.) This scoring system may be applied to Pitch (below) and California Jack (page 33).

Pitch. Pitch is a bidding form of All Fours, and for this reason it is generally known as Auction Pitch, more usually played by four than by two. Starting with the non-dealer, each in turn bids to gain a minimum number of game points (High, Low, Jack and Game, as before) in exchange for the right of nominating trumps. Whoever bids the higher number establishes trumps by leading or 'pitching' a card of that suit, which starts the play. Both players score what they actually win, but the pitcher, if he fails to win as many as he bid, is set back by the amount of his bid – *ie*, that amount is deducted from his score. From this feature, the game is also known as Setback.

4 DRAW GAMES
German Whist – California Jack – Honeymoon Bridge etc

Two-hand card game anthologies usually devote separate sections to the games listed above. Such games, however, are for the most part makeshift adaptations for two players of trick-taking games more frequently and more smoothly played by four, or some other number. All are based on the same method of changing four hands of 13 cards each into two hands of 26, by adopting the 'draw' principle as follows:

Deal so many cards each, and place the remainder face down to form a stock. After playing the first trick in the usual way, the winner of the trick draws the top card of the stock and adds it to his hand, waits for his opponent to draw the next, then leads to the second trick. After each trick there is a draw in the same way. When all stock cards have been drawn, the cards remaining in hand are played out to tricks until neither has any left. Thus 26 tricks will have been played in all.

It will be observed that almost any favourite trick-taking game can be played by two players in this way, the rules and scoring of the basic game being applied to the procedure described above. There is one flaw in the whole idea, and that is that the rule requiring the second player to follow suit to the card led is unenforceable during the first half of the game, as there is no way of telling whether or not the second has revoked. No matter how much you trust your opponent, or even yourself, it strikes me that a game so open to temptation on the one hand and suspicion on the other can hardly be played with complete equanimity. The most practical way of overcoming this fault in the underlying principle is to introduce the rule followed at Bézique, which is that the second player need not follow suit but may play as he wishes. This rule ceases, of course, once the stock is exhausted.

German Whist

In this game only six cards are dealt to each player. The top card of the stock is turned face up and establishes the trump suit for the whole of that game. The object of play is to win the majority of tricks. Non-dealer leads to the first trick. The second player must follow suit if he can; otherwise he may win by trumping or lose by playing any other card. The trick-winner draws the top card of stock, which is faced, and the loser draws the next. Before leading, the winner faces the next card of the stock so that both may see what it is before the trick is played. The game is a tie if both take 13 tricks.

The most interesting feature of German Whist is the fact that the next stock card is visible. If it is a good card, both players will try to win the trick; if not, they may seek to lose in the hope of drawing a better one from immediately beneath it.

A variation in play, which rather spoils the point of seeing the top card, requires the trick-loser to show his opponent what card he has drawn. It may be preferred by those who like games that exercise memory rather than judgement.

California Jack

This is the draw version of All Fours (page 26). As at German Whist, deal six cards each and turn up the top card of the stock to establish trumps. The winner of each trick draws the top (faced) card of stock and his opponent draws the second (unseen), and the next card is faced again before the next trick is led by the previous winner.

The rules of play and scoring features are as at All Fours, All Fives or Pitch, except that normal Whist rules of trick-play apply – *ie* the second player must follow suit if he can. (A nonsensical rule, for reasons already stated.) One point each is scored for winning High, Low, Jack and Game, as explained on page 27, and the winner is the first to reach a total of 10 points in as many deals as it takes.

Honeymoon Bridge

This game is only recommended for Bridge addicts and a knowledge of Bridge is assumed in this explanation. Deal 13 cards each and form a stock of the remainder. No card of the stock is ever seen except by one player, when he draws and adds it to his hand after a trick is played. During the first part of the game, when it is still possible to draw from stock, tricks are played at no trump and it is obligatory to follow suit. The first 13 tricks are of no account to the score. When they are over, there being no stock and each holding 13 cards in his final hand, the dealer may either bid or pass. Bidding proceeds as at Contract Bridge (or any other form of Bridge as preferred), and a contract is established when a bid, double or redouble is followed by a pass. The defender (non-bidder) leads, and the game is then played and scored as at Bridge. Official rules quote a penalty for revoking during the first half of the game, but do not explain how the fault can be proved other than by self-confession or the employment of an umpire.

5 CASSINO

There is a distinct family of card games that involves neither playing tricks as in the majority of games, nor collecting sets and sequences as in Rummy, Poker and a large number of others. We might call them 'sweeping games', as the object is to capture cards from the table by matching them with cards played from the hand, and a special score is usually given to 'sweeping the board', which means capturing all the table cards in one fell swoop (or sweep). The whole family is distinctly Mediterranean in flavour and probably of Italian origin, its chief member being Italy's national card game Scopone, for four players.

Of this family, the essentially two-handed Cassino is the 'one that got away' and has most found favour with the English-speaking card world on both sides of the Atlantic, though more on the western than the eastern side, no doubt because of the Italianate population of America. No matter how carefully an account is phrased, Cassino always looks complicated at first reading. Once you start playing, you may at first find it so simple as to be trivial. Closer acquaintance, however, soon reveals hidden depths to the play.

Cassino has long been spelt with a double S. Recent books state that this is a misspelling for Casino, and revert to the 'correct' spelling. I retain the misspelling, which may be regarded as now sanctioned by usage, to avoid any possible ambiguity, as a Cassino game is by no stretch of the imagination a casino game.

There are several variations to the game and the most basic form is described first.

The game

Cards. A standard 52-card pack.

Card values. Each Ace counts as 1, other numerals as face value. Courts do not have values.

Deal. After agreeing who goes first and then shuffling and cutting, deal two cards face down to your opponent, two to the table, two to yourself, and the same again. Each player takes his four cards into hand, and the four table cards are turned face up and arranged in a row. The rest of the pack is put face down to one side to form a stock.

Object. The object at each turn is to capture one or more table cards by matching it (them) in certain prescribed ways with a card played from the hand. If the card played from hand cannot properly match, it is left on the table and so increases the number of cards available for capture. If the card from hand captures all cards on the table, it is called a sweep and scores a bonus. Each player lays his captured and capturing cards face down in a pile, and at the end of the game scores for having:

more cards than the opponent	3
more spades than the opponent	1
♢T, known as Big Cassino	2
♠2, known as Little Cassino	1
each Ace captured	1
each sweep made	1

In brief, the object is to capture as many cards as possible, especially Aces, spades, and the Ten of diamonds.

Play. Each player at each turn plays a card from the hand face up to the table, and may or may not capture as explained below. When neither has any cards left, the same dealer deals four more (in pairs) to each player from the top of the stock, but no more to the table. When the last round is being dealt, the dealer must announce that it is the last.

In playing a card to the table, a player may do one of the following:

1. Capture by pairing, combining or both.
2. Build pairs or totals for subsequent capture.
3. Increase such builds, whether made by himself or his opponent.
4. Trail (none of the above).

Capturing (*'Taking in'*). A court card played from the hand may capture one table card of the same rank by pairing: a King captures a King, and so on.

Numeral cards also capture by pairing, but can capture as many of the same rank as may be available: an Ace can capture one or more Aces, and so on.

Numeral cards, furthermore, can capture by combining. That is, two or more single cards on the table may be captured by playing from hand a card equal to their combined values. For example, a Ten can capture an Ace and a Nine, or two Fives, or two Threes and a Four, and so on.

One numeral card may make as many captures as it can in one turn by pairing and/or combining. But table cards which have been grouped together in builds, as described below, can be captured only as builds, not as individual cards.

Building. Numerical cards (not courts) can be played from the hand in conjunction with cards on the table to form builds for capture on subsequent turns. This may be done by pairing or combining.

> *A pairing example:* If you hold two Fives and there is a Five on the table, you can play one from hand upon the one on the table (announcing 'Building Fives'), then capture both by pairing on your next turn – unless, that is, your opponent held the fourth Five and himself captured them on his intervening turn.
>
> *A combining example:* If there were a Five on the table and you held a Three and an Eight, you could on one turn play the Three upon the Five (announcing 'Building eight'), and on your next turn use your Eight to capture the build, along with any other captures that may be open to it.

It is obligatory to announce what build is being made, as this could otherwise cause confusion. For instance, if one player plays a Five upon a Five and announces 'Building Fives', that build can be captured only by a Five; but if he announces 'Building ten', it can be captured only by a Ten.

You may only make a build if you are able to capture or increase it on your next turn.

Increasing builds. A pairing build can be increased by the addition of another card of the same rank. For example, if you held three Fives and there were one on the table, you could build one on your first turn, add another on your second, then capture them all on your third.

A combined-total build may be increased by the addition of another card from hand, provided that you hold a card that can be used to capture it on the next turn. For example: Opponent plays a Two to a Three, announces 'Building five', thereby indicating that he can capture it on his next turn with a Five from the hand. You, holding an Ace and a Six, add the Ace to that build and announce 'Building six', hoping that he himself cannot immediately capture with a Six, or increase it further.

It is not permitted to increase a multiple build. For example, if one player builds fours with a Four, a Three and an Ace, the other may not add a Two and announce 'Building ten'. He could do so, however, if the other had declared that combination to represent eight instead of fours when he built it.

A build may be increased only by the addition of a card from the hand, not with one already on the table.

Trailing. If a player cannot or will not take in, build or increase, he 'trails' by playing any card face up to the table, thereby adding to the cards available for capture. But a player may not trail if any build he made is still on the table.

Sweeps. If a player sweeps the board by capturing all the table cards with a single card from his hand, he is credited with making a sweep. To indicate this fact, he should place the card he captured face up (instead of down) on his pile of won cards. At the end of the game, sweeps can then be counted by scoring for each face up card. After a sweep, the opponent can only trail.

End of game. The game ends when there are no cards in stock and both have played out their cards from the hand. Any cards left on the table at the end of play are credited to the player who last made a capture. This does not in itself count as a sweep, though it is possible for the last move of a game to be a valid sweep in the usual way.

FIGURE 2

North, to move, can immediately capture the table Three by pairing with the Three from his hand. But he can do better by adding his Two to the table Ace and announcing 'Building Threes', adding the table Three to that build. On his next turn he can use his hand Three to capture all three cards (♢A, ♢2, ♡3). If it were South's move, he could add his Four to the Three, announce 'Building Sevens', and on his next turn capture ♣4, ♡3 and ♠7 with his ♡7. But after North's build, he cannot add the Four to either of the Threes and announce 'Sevens' because the multiple build of Threes can only be captured by a Three. Nor could he capture ♢A+ ♠7 with his ♠8, as ♢A forms part of a build and cannot be taken individually.

Score. Each player sorts through his cards and scores according to the table on page 36. If there is a tie for 'cards' neither scores for that feature. Each deal is regarded as a complete game when two play.

Variants

Cassino is subject to several variations in play, some of which have special names. In the basic game as described above, it may be agreed that if three court cards of the same rank are on the table, a player holding the fourth may capture them all. Sweeps are often ignored in two-hand play. (The game is frequently played by three or four.) The following three variants can be combined in the same game, if desired.

Draw Cassino. Immediately after each turn, each player draws the top card of the stock to restore his hand to four cards. This dispenses with making separate deals of four at a time.

Royal Cassino. Jack counts 11, Queen 12, King 13, and Ace either 1 or 14 as specified by the player. The restrictions on court cards do not then apply, and they are used in exactly the same way as numerals. Sometimes Little Cassino scores 2 or 15 to whoever captures it, and Big Cassino 10 or 16. (Optional.)

Spade Cassino. This replaces the blanket score of 1 for capturing more spades by crediting points for capturing individual spades. The Ace, Two and Jack of spades count 2 each to whoever holds them at the end of play, and every other spade counts 1 point. As this increases the maximum possible score from 11 to 26, the game is often played up to 61 and scored on a Cribbage board. If the loser fails to reach 31, the winner's margin of victory is doubled.

6 SPITE AND MALICE

This fast and furious game seems to be a modern development of such competitive patiences as Russian Bank (Crapette) and Racing Demon (Race Canfield, or Pounce), and the name – very descriptive, as will be seen – may be older than the game, as I have heard it apply to Racing Demon. I nearly avoided referring to it as a form of competitive patience, as there are some card-players who dislike the one-player activity and get put off by the word itself. So let us be quite clear from the outset that this is not a simple case of each player having a game of patience and seeing which one comes out first. This is a real two-player game offering every opportunity for the exercise of – well, spite and malice; and in the long run it will always be won by the more spiteful and malicious of the two.

The game

Cards. Two full packs are used. They should be of the same size and format, but of differing back designs or colours, and are not to be shuffled together at the outset. One of these packs should contain the standard 52 cards, the other a total of 56 cards by the addition of four Jokers. Ideally, the four Jokers should be of the same back design/colour and thus indistinguishable from the rest of their pack. In practice, since most packs contain only two Jokers or at most three, it doesn't matter too much if two Jokers are used from the other pack. This works out better than dispensing with one Joker if a three-Joker pack is used.

Deal. Both packs must be very thoroughly shuffled before play. The importance of this cannot be over-emphasised, as poor shuffling ruins the game. The 52-card pack is divided evenly, each player receiving 26 cards face down. Five cards each are dealt from the second pack, the rest of which is placed face down to one side to form a stock. Each player squares up his 26-card pack, placing it to his right (or left if he is left-handed), and turning the top card of it face up. This pile of cards is his personal pack, and will be referred to here simply as his 'pack', the central pile being known as the 'stock'. The other five cards he takes up as his playing hand.

Object. Each player's object is to be the first to get rid of his pack by playing out all 26 cards to the table, one by one as the opportunity arises. The first to do so automatically ends the game and scores 1 point for each card left in his opponent's pack. This is the sole object: there is no score for doing anything else.

Rank of cards. Cards rank A 2 3 4 5 6 7 8 9 T J Q K. Suits have no significance in the play. Jokers are wild. The holder of a Joker may declare it to represent any rank he pleases and play it as if it were a card of that rank.

Play. The first move is made by the player whose pack has the higher-ranking upcard. (If the upcards are of the same rank, each player shuffles his pack and turns up the top card again.) A move consists of transferring a card from one place to another, and a turn may consist of as many moves as the player is able and willing to make. Few moves are compulsory, and the decision whether to move or not is sometimes a tricky point of strategy. It sometimes happens that one player is unable to move at his turn, or unwilling to do so, in which case the other may take a number of turns in succession.

If the first player holds an Ace he may play it to the centre of the table. Upon this he may play a Two if he has one, upon the Two a Three, and so on, such cards coming either from his hand or from the top of his pack. Each time he plays a card from the top of his pack, he immediately faces the one beneath. Throughout play, any Ace played to the centre of the table forms the base of a pile of cards which is gradually to be built up in sequence as far as the King, regardless of suit. The only way in which either player may reduce his pack is by playing off the upcard to one of these centre piles at the appropriate point. We will call these centre piles 'stacks'.[1]

If the starter has no Ace, or is unwilling to play one, or is otherwise unable to proceed further, he may finish his play by discarding one card face up to the table in front of him. He may not make more than one discard, but is not obliged to make any. He completes his turn by drawing from the top of the stock as many as he needs to restore his hand to five.

It is then the turn of the second player. If his upcard is an Ace he is obliged to start a stack with it; if it is a Two, he is obliged to stack it upon an Ace if one is available; if it is anything else, he is not obliged to stack it (but will be advised to do so if he can). Apart from that, he may start and add to as many stacks as he is able and willing to, and may complete his turn by making one discard before drawing from the stock to restore his hand to five.

Play continues in this way, but with the following added feature. Each player may start up to four discard piles altogether, and may make subsequent discards to any of his own piles, provided that the card it is played upon is of the same rank or one rank higher. (Example: If the first card of a pile is a King, subsequent discards may run: Q J J J T 9 9 8, and so on.) It is never permissible to discard an Ace. The top card of a discard pile is always available for playing to a stack.

Whenever a player succeeds in playing all five cards from his hand, he is entitled to another turn immediately upon drawing five more cards from stock.

Other rules governing play are as follows.

Replenishing stock. No more cards may be added to a stack when it has been built up to the King. Whenever the stock is depleted to fewer than 12 cards, it is replenished by taking all the stacks that have been built up to the King and shuffling them in with the stock. Since some of these cards will be those played off the personal packs, the number of cards available from stock gradually increases during the play. If no stacks have been

1. Patience games lack an adequate word for this feature. 'Foundation' is inaccurate, and 'centre pile' long-winded.

completed by the time the stock is exhausted, all the stacks that have been started are gathered up, shuffled, and turned to form the new stock. (The importance of thorough shuffling at these points cannot be overemphasised. The best way of carrying it out is to put the stacks together, deal a row of six or seven cards face down, then another row on top of that, and so on until they are all out. Then pick up the piles in random order, shuffle them once or twice, and place the whole pile beneath the few cards remaining in stock.)

Compulsory/optional play. The following moves, when possible, are compulsory. If a player's upcard is an Ace he must use it to start a stack. If an Ace is available on the table, waiting to be built upon, the player in turn must cover it if his upcard is a Two, or if a Two is visible among his discards (though in this case he *may* cover it from the hand instead). If a player is unable to play, he must pass his turn without compensation. If he is unwilling to play, he may say 'pass' and allow his opponent an extra turn as often as he likes. If both players pass, the first to do so must then play an Ace or a Two from his hand if he can, and his opponent must then do likewise. For this purpose, however, it is not compulsory to play a Joker as such if no Ace or Two is held. If both players are still unable or unwilling to play further, *all* cards in hand and on the table (except the private packs) are gathered up and shuffled together. The new stock is turned down, five more cards are dealt to each, and play begins again as if from scratch.

Jokers. When a Joker is discarded, its holder need not specify which rank it represents until he needs to do so. For example, if the top card of a discard pile is a Nine, and two Jokers are added to it, they may be followed by a Nine, Eight, Seven or Six. A Joker may not be discarded upon a Two[2]. No matter what a Joker represents when it lies on a discard pile, it may be played to a stack at any time, or used as an Ace to start a new one.

---

2. This rule, which causes no hardship, is here recommended to overcome inconsistencies and points of argument that might otherwise arise. The need to invoke it rarely occurs.

Score. Play ceases as soon as one player has played his last up-card, and he scores 1 point for every card left unplayed from his opponent's pack. As there is a natural tendency to play at least three games to a session, here are some suggestions for spicing up the game score:

1. A rubber is won by the first player to win two games, and a bonus of 10 is added for the rubber.
2. Three games are played, and the margin of victory is the difference between the two totals; but if the second and third games are won by the same player his total is doubled (unless this results in a tie).
3. Three games are played, and the winner of a game scores the number of cards in his opponent's pack multiplied by the face value of his upcard (counting numerals at face value, courts 10 each and Ace 11).
4. Three games are played, and the winner of a game scores 100 plus the total face value of all cards remaining in his oppon-ant's pack (counting as above).
5. The Hollywood scoring system devised for Gin Rummy may be used – see page 20.

Other elements of variety might be introduced by (a) permitting a player to resign, in which case his opponent scores the difference between the total of cards left in the two packs, and (b) offering 'double or quits' as in the game of Le Truc (p. 123). The first possibility should be governed by some sort of control against indiscriminate resignation, *eg* by allowing the winner a minimum score of 10.

Suggestions for play

You may find the game gets off to a slow start. This is quite normal, and it will invariably pick up speed later. What often happens is that neither player is dealt an Ace or a Joker, and for several turns the only thing each can do is make a discard and draw one from stock. Even this may get held up. One, for example, may find himself unable to discard after a few turns, in which case he has no choice but to wait until the other has changed the situation by inaugurating a stack. Or again, if one player's upcard is low, say a Three, the other may well hold back the play of an Ace until he can play A–2–3 and so block that opening. Although it is undeniably disadvantageous (not to say annoying) for one player to be stuck this early in the game, allowing the other to play off perhaps half a dozen or more upcards, the possible swings of fortune are such as to give him a fair chance of catching up later.

It is worth noting that, as Aces get played off, the number of potential stacks increases from the original eight (Aces and Jokers) to a maximum of twelve. At a later stage in the game a position is usually reached from which there are so many stacks at different stages of construction that one may be able to play off anything up to ten upcards in succession. It may also be useful to know that at the very start of play there is a slightly better than 1 in 6 chance of drawing any given rank or a Joker, a figure liable to considerable fluctuation as play progresses. It is therefore a marked advantage to be able to play out all five cards from the hand, as you have an immediate second turn with about a 5-in-6 chance of drawing a desired card. Not only should you never miss an opportunity to play out all five, but also you should often refrain from play if there is a chance of reaching this position. For example, holding A–2–3–5–9, you may prefer to discard the Nine and hope to draw a Four (or Joker) rather than play A–2–3 for a new stack. Of course, this principle may be unwise to follow in certain positions. But it quite often happens that a player manages to clear his hand two or three times in succession, and this will always do him more good than harm.

Given the choice, you should prefer to play to a stack (1) from the top of your pack, or, if not possible, (2) from your hand, and only then (3) from your discards. Since the whole object of the game is to empty your pack, while nothing else counts, you should never miss an opportunity to play the upcard, remembering to turn the next one *immediately*, in case it will also go. It is worth playing from your pack even if it gives your opponent an opening too. Perhaps the only time this does not apply is when it gives him a certain play-off and he is considerably in the lead. But whenever you are in the lead, or there is not much in it, always play the upcard when you can.

With the choice of playing from hand or discards, it is usually desirable in principle to play from the hand, as this enables you to draw from stock and so keep up a constant throughput of varying cards. Sometimes, of course, you must play from the discards in order to run through a sequence, and it is usually better to play from the discards in order to get rid of a kink – *ie* two or more consecutive cards of the same rank preventing access to other cards beneath them. For example, with a pile consisting of 9–8–7–6–5–5 it would be better to play a Five from the table than from the hand, unless perhaps you could otherwise clear the hand and have another turn. (Incidentally, in my circle we spread each discard pile to form a column of overlapping cards so that all are visible, in which case the word 'pile' is not strictly accurate. If they are kept as piles so that underlying cards are not visible, the skill of the game becomes that of memory rather than calculation. Which is preferable is a matter of taste.)

With no choice but to play a discard to a stack, do not bother to do so unless it brings some advantage. It may, for example, enable you to continue with a card from hand or even the upcard, or empty a discard pile to make room for a new one, or build a stack up to the same rank as that of your opponent's upcard, or perhaps raise several stacks to the same level where this looks as if it will hinder him more than yourself. But don't build a stack up to the King just because you can, nor higher than you need in order to block your adversary. Otherwise you may, after next playing your upcard, turn a rank which *could* have been played had you not previously blocked it by purposeless building.

The true test of skill in Spite and Malice lies in the management of discard piles. Never discard without carefully considering the likely consequences: one bad move can hold you up for a long time. The important thing to remember is that you are not obliged to discard, and it is sometimes better to refrain from doing so, especially to avoid creating a kink. A tricky situation often arises in which the only available move involves making a doubtful discard; the question is then whether to make it for the sake of drawing from stock, or to leave it and perhaps allow your opponent several consecutive turns. You just have to play it by ear.

If the game is a long time in starting, with neither player able (or willing) to stack an Ace, do not worry overmuch about using up all four of your depots. Later, however, it is desirable to restrict them to three for as long as possible, in order to leave space for the eventual transfer of a card or cards vital to your game. A positive example would be if you held A–3–4–5–K and your upcard were a Six, in which case you would open a column with the Five and hope to pick up a Two as you built downwards. A negative example would be if you suddenly found yourself drawing third or fourth cards of the same (and useless) rank, in which case you would have to use up that space as a dumping ground for them.

We have already noted that kinks consisting of several consecutive cards of the same rank can be a distinct hindrance to your game, and should therefore be avoided as much as possible. This only applies, of course, where kinks are obscuring access to other cards, and it follows that a run of identical cards can be quite safely played as the base of a discard pile, since they obscure nothing. A good rank to start a pile with is therefore one of which you hold two or three, as you are guaranteed a discard – and a draw from stock – for several turns to come without spoiling your game. If you lack duplicates, it is best to open a pile with the top card of a sequence. For example, holding 2–5–6–7–Q, drop the Seven first, as it assures you of three consecutive discards and draws. Note that it is not important to start all piles with the highest rank possible. Four Kings, for example, are better discarded as the base of one pile than as the bases of four. The ideal arrangement is to run four piles from different bases – say K, J, 8, 5 – so as to maximise your chances of discarding any given rank.

Having started a descending sequence, try to avoid creating a kink by the play of a duplicate. If one duplicate becomes necessary, forming a single kink, do not worry too much as a subsequent play-off as far as the first will unblock the sequence for a later move. But it is usually disastrous to play two or more duplicates in mid-sequence, causing a double or multiple kink, as you will then have to devote as much energy to unkinking it as to playing your upcards, which is self-defeating. The higher-ranking the duplicates are, the more difficult it is to get rid of them: at a pinch, you can allow a run of Twos or perhaps Threes, as it is rarely profitable for either player (hence your opponent) to constipate his hand by holding back Aces and Twos, since the former cannot be discarded and the latter must be played off if no other move is open to either player.

It is useful to stop a sequence at the card next in rank above your own upcard. Suppose that you are trying to play off a Six, that you hold 2–3–6–J–Q, that you have three current discard piles of which one runs T T T 9 8 7, and that you are unable to discard except to the empty depot. In this case you will discard your Six (in hand) not to the Seven but to the spare depot. If you subsequently find yourself able to play off your Six, and then turn up 8, 9, T, J, Q or K, you will be able to play that off with the aid of your sequence, which you would not have been able to do had you blocked it with the Six. This is a good example of the need for a spare discard pile, and hence of the value of clearing out a discard pile whenever you can do so without incurring any tactical disadvantage.

Jokers require careful management too. It is certainly an advantage to be able to discard one without specifying which rank it represents, and then be able to stack it as any other rank you please. Personally, however, I go to every length to avoid wasting a Joker on a discard pile. In my view the primary purpose of a Joker is to enable the upcard to be played. Keep Jokers in your hand for as long as you can, and use them only (and immediately) as part of a sequence leading to the play of your upcard. One other reasonable use of a Joker is to enable you to play out all five cards from hand and draw five more for another turn, though I would not myself use *two* Jokers for this purpose. A Joker on a discard pile is a drawback for two reasons.

First, your opponent can see it, and will adjust his play accordingly, thus lessening its power. Second, you may be forced to cover it with another discard, and once this is done there follows a period during which you might as well not have it at all. Another good way of wasting a Joker is to count it as an Ace and stack it for no other reason than that there was nothing else to do.

Despite all these thoughts about playing off your own upcard, don't forget that at least half your game lies in preventing your opponent from doing the same. Never make a move without examining his upcard, the uppermost stack-cards, the cards which you can see to be available to him in his own discard columns, and the possible cards he holds. Or, as more often applies, the ranks he possibly lacks from his hand. For instance, if his upcard is a Seven, and he keeps discarding and drawing when one of the stacks goes up to Five, then it is evident that he lacks a Six and a Joker from his hand. You, therefore, will avoid stacking a Six until you can cover it with a Seven, and will lose no opportunity to build any stack up to the Seven – perhaps even using a Joker for the purpose if the situation is critical. If several piles are stacked to the Four or Five, and you have low cards to get rid of, it is often worth building up lower stacks to the same rank. If he is going to be able to play anyway once he has drawn a Six, he might as well have half a dozen stacks open to him as two or three.

If his upcard is high – let's say a King – and all the stacks are fairly low, look carefully at his discards and note how many ranks he needs in hand to be able to run up a sequence to the King. For instance, he may have visible access to 6, 7, 8 and T, J. In this case, you would avoid building up to a Five as there is a fair chance that he holds a Nine and Queen (or Joker), but you might build up to a Four, banking on his not holding all three missing ranks.

To summarise, the most important requirements of the game are to keep your eyes open and your wits about you, and never to play a single card without a thorough appraisal of the consequences likely to proceed from it.

PART II
GAMES WITH A SHORT PACK

Many games of European origin are played with a short pack of only 32 cards. Such packs, which are easily obtainable on the continent, may be duplicated by removing all the ranks lower than Seven from a 52-card pack. Some games of this type require several short packs shuffled together; some are played with even shorter packs of only 24 cards (nothing lower than Nine in each suit). All those described here are of the trick-taking variety, though Bézique is not so much about tricks as about collecting matched cards, as in Rummy. Beginners are recommended to embark upon Ecarté first in order to get used to the short pack and to the principles of trick-play. Piquet is the most classic game; Bézique the most romantic; Sixty Six the shortest; Klabberjass the most widely played; Ecarté the simplest and Le Truc the funniest.

7 PIQUET

The odd thing about Piquet is that although it is widely regarded as the best of all two-hand card games by those in a position to judge, it is nowadays almost equally widely neglected. Not a hundred years ago it was still the everyday card game of the French, occupying in many respects a position equivalent to that of Cribbage in England, but has now ceded pride of place to that Gallic form of Klabberjass called Belote. For many periods between the 17th century and the First World War, though by fits and starts rather than continuously, Piquet found itself a favourite of the English moneyed classes, lying second perhaps only to Whist and later Bridge. American ignorance of the game is and always has been total.

Yet Piquet is a game unlike any other. Unique in format, it is richly varied, unfailingly exciting, and demanding of the highest skills. It has been neglected, I think, partly because like so many other fine card games it has been swept aside by the single-minded tyranny of Bridge; perhaps partly because it looks complicated at first sight and calls for the constant application of even more mental arithmetic than Cribbage (in which connection it may be noted that Cribbage boards are easily obtainable but Piquet markers are now antiques); even, possibly, because it is full of French technical terms which are not pronounced as they are spelt. More probably there is no reason at all, except to say that Piquet is out of fashion. There are fashions in all things, and card games are not excepted.

Pronounced 'picket' in English and 'P.K.' in France, Piquet is traditionally regarded as a French invention and equally traditionally dated back to the 15th century. In fact, legend attributes it to the genius of a certain Stephen de Vignoles, one of Charles VII's chevaliers who, under the title La Hire, is perpetuated to this day as the Jack of hearts in French 'named' packs. (♡K is Charles and ♡Q Judith.) A hundred years later

Rabelais listed the game as one of those played by Gargantua. It was formerly known as Cent, anglicised to Sant or Saunt, from the circumstance of being played 100 up – *ie* the winner was the first player to reach 100 points. The version described below, however, is that known as Rubicon Piquet, as formulated in 1882 by the Portland Club (once the *académie anglaise* of the card world; now given over to Bridge). The 'rubicon' is the scoring of 100 points, but the improvement over the old game lies in the fact that a fixed number of deals are played and the loser is heavily penalised if he fails to cross the Rubicon by reaching 100.

The game

Equipment. At least one pack of 32 cards, consisting of A K Q J T 9 8 7 in each suit. (It is convenient to use two packs, one being shuffled while the other is dealt.) One scoresheet, or one each, and something to write with. Optionally, some form of scorer or marker capable of indicating from 1 to 200 points at least. A proper Piquet marker is illustrated, but a Cribbage board can be turned to use. Serious players announce their cumulative scores verbally as play proceeds, and beginners should aim to dispense with mechanical aids as soon as they know the game.

General idea. A game (or *partie*, to use the needless French word) consists of six deals, and is won by the player with the higher cumulative score. Both players strive to make at least 100 points, as the loser is heavily penalised if he fails to do so. In the event of a draw two more deals are played. It is worth knowing in advance that a player may score anything from zero to 170 on a single deal, but that, on *average*, elder hand (non-dealer) expects to make about 28 to younger's 14 or so. Each deal consists of two parts. In the first, each player throws out some of his cards and draws others from the pack in an attempt to score for acquiring certain combinations of cards. In the second, these cards are played out to tricks at no trump, and the object is normally to win a majority of the twelve tricks. Most of the skill lies in selecting which cards to throw out, but much may also be expended on, if not actually winning the majority of tricks, at least dividing them six-all.

Deal. Whoever cuts the higher card may elect to deal first, and is advised to do so. Thereafter, the turn to deal alternates, so that each deals three times in the course of a game. The dealer is known as younger hand, his opponent as elder. Deal 12 cards each in batches of three at a time (or, if preferred, two at a time; but whichever a player uses on his first deal he must stick to for the rest of the game). Place the remaining eight cards face down in the centre of the table, forming the stock (or *talon*); they should be spread slightly, so that all are easily accessible.

Carte blanche. If either player's hand contains no court cards (Kings, Queens or Jacks), he is entitled to score 10 points for carte blanche provided that he announces this fact before any discarding takes place. He must also prove it by rapidly playing his cards one by one and face up into a pile, but this not until his opponent has discarded for the exchange. If younger has it, therefore, he announces it immediately, waits for elder to discard, and then proves it. If elder has it, he announces it immediately, tells younger how many cards he proposes to leave him in the exchange, waits for younger to make his discard accordingly, and then proves it. (The point of this ritual is that a player is entitled to see his opponent's carte blanche, but not to be influenced by it in deciding upon his discards. In any case, carte blanche is an extremely rare occurrence. The English for carte blanche, by the way, is 'a blank'.

The exchange. The object of the exchange is to improve the hand for the purpose of (a) winning tricks at no trump, and (b) acquiring the best scoring combination of cards in each of these three classes:

Point Most cards in one suit.
Sequence Longest sequence in one suit.
Set Three, or (preferably) four, Aces, K, Q, J or Tens.

Both players are obliged to exchange at least one card. Elder starts by discarding, face down, anything from one to five cards, and drawing the same number from the top of the stock consecutively downwards. If he exchanges fewer than five, he may look at those of the top five which he did not take, without showing them to younger. Younger then discards up to as many as there are left in the stock – usually only three – and similarly replaces them from the top of the stock down. If he leaves any in stock, he may not (yet) see what they are.

Declaring (*and sinking*). The principle is that 'point' is scored only by the player with the longer or better suit, sequences only by the player with the longest or highest, and sets only by the player with the higher-ranking quatorze (four of a kind) or trio (three) if no quatorze is held. The method is that elder announces his best combination in each class, and younger tells him whether or not he can beat it. Any combination eventually scored for must be fully identified, if not actually shown. But a player is not obliged to declare any combination that he holds, or to declare the whole of it if he does. The practice of keeping any part of it back (and of course losing the right to score for it) is known as 'sinking'. It is an advanced tactic and may be ignored for the moment.

Point. Elder first states the number of cards in his longest suit. To this, younger replies 'not good' if he has a longer suit, 'good' if his best suit is shorter. If equal, he asks elder its total face value ('making?'), to which elder replies on the basis of adding together 11 for the Ace, 10 for each court, face value for each numeral. If younger's point is of equal value, he says 'equal' and neither may score for point. If elder's point is acknowledged 'good', he scores 1 point per card in that suit, announces what the suit is (and the cards composing it if requested) and passes on to the next declaration.

Sequence. A sequence is three or more cards of the same suit and of consecutive ranks. The six possible sequences and their scoring values are:

tierce (three)	= 3	sixieme (six)	=16
quart (four)	= 4	septieme (seven)	=17
quint (five)	=15	huitieme (eight)	=18

Elder announces the length of his longest sequence, to which younger replies 'good' if he cannot beat it, 'not good' if he has a longer sequence, or 'top card?' if his best sequence is of the same length. In the latter event, elder states the highest card of his sequence, which again younger acknowledges good, not good or equal. If equal, neither player may score for any sequences. If good, elder identifies and scores for all the sequences he may hold.

Set. Finally, elder announces his highest-ranking quatorze (four of the same rank) by saying 'fourteen Aces' or whatever the rank may be, or, if none, his highest-ranking trio ('three Aces', and so on). Any quatorze beats a trio, and a higher-ranking set beats a lower set of the same type. As the names imply, a quatorze scores 14 and a trio 3 points. If younger has a superior set he replies 'not good'. If not, he replies 'good' (equality is impossible), after which elder identifies and scores for as many sets as he holds. Remember that ranks below Ten are not valid as sets.

One for leading. At this juncture, elder announces his total score for combinations so far (if any), leads any card to the first trick, and adds one point for doing so. There is no reason for this: it is just a rule of the game.

Younger's declarations. After elder has led, but before younger replies to it, the latter declares and scores for any combinations he may hold in classes to which he replied 'not good', or which elder passed over because he had nothing to declare. First, however, he must decide whether or not to look at any cards he may have left untaken from the stock, and announce this decision. If yes, he may reveal them to both players at any time until he plays to the first trick, but not after. If he sees them, so may elder; if not, neither may elder. As to his own combinations, younger must count them in the same order as elder. For point, he announces the suit and scores 1 per card in it. For sequence and then for set, he must declare and score for at least one that is better than any claimed by elder, and may also declare and score for any others he may hold. He is then ready to play to the first trick – but there are still two scoring features that may apply, as follows.

Repique. If either player reaches or exceeds a score of 30 for combinations alone before his opponent has scored anything at all, he adds to his score a bonus of 60 for 'repique'. The fact that elder declares before younger is not an advantage, because scores accrue strictly in the following order: carte blanche, point, sequence, set. Thus if younger counted 10 for carte blanche, 6 for point and a quint for 15, he would have reached 31 in time to score repique (making 91) even if elder had managed to score for sets. Equality does not save a repique. If both have the same point and neither scores for sequence, two quatorzes and a trio will win the repique.

Pique. If elder reaches 30+ before younger has scored anything at all, not on combinations alone (which would be repique) but including his one for leading and any other points for subsequently won tricks as may be necessary, he adds to his score a bonus of 30 for pique. Thus if younger has scored nothing for combinations, he must win a trick before elder reaches 30 to avoid being piqued. Younger himself cannot score pique, because if he fails to make 30 on combinations alone elder is bound to score at least one 'for leading'.

Tricks. It is obligatory to follow suit to the card led if possible; if not, any other card may be played but will lose the trick. There are no trumps, and the trick is won by the higher-ranking card of the suit led. The winner of a trick adds 1 or 2 points to his score and announces his cumulative total to date, and leads to the next. Score 1 point for winning a trick led by oneself, 2 points for capturing a trick led by the opponent.[3] Won tricks

---

3. The usual way of expressing the score for tricks is: 'One for leading to a trick, one for capturing an opponent's lead, and one for winning the last trick'. This comes to exactly the same thing.

may be left face up on the table, as either player is entitled to refer to any or all cards already played, as well as to his own discards.

Score for cards. If both players win six tricks, the cards are said to be divided, and neither scores any bonus. For winning a majority of tricks, there is a bonus of 10 'for the cards', and for winning all twelve there is an additional bonus of 30 for 'capot'.[4] Neither of these bonuses counts towards pique.

Scoring. At the end of the deal, each player announces his cumulative total for it, and these figures are entered on the score-sheet. At the end of the sixth deal, each player's scores are totalled, and the higher wins a game score determined as follows. If the loser has 100 or more, the winner scores 100 plus the difference between the two totals (*eg* 196 to 173 wins 123). If the loser failed to reach 100, he is rubiconed, and the winner

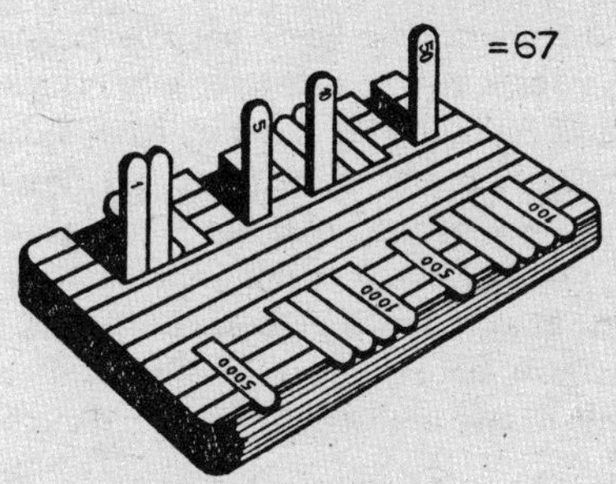

FIGURE 3

Piquet markers dating from about the turn of the century may still be found in antique shops or even junk stalls. They were made in pairs (one for each player) and consisted of spring-loaded pegs set into an oblong of polished wood of about the size of a playing card. A score is recorded by raising the appropriate peg or combination of pegs. The one illustrated here was also designed for use in the game of Bézique, in which scores range from 5 to over 5000.

4. Usually expressed as '40 for capot instead of 10 for cards', which comes to the same thing but disfigures the logic of the game.

scores 100 plus the addition of the two totals (*e.g.* 96 to 73 wins 269). It is not incumbent upon the winner to cross the rubicon. In the event of a tie, two more deals may be played, and if this does not resolve it the game is drawn. An alternative tie-break (proposed by myself) is to credit a game score of 100 to whichever player was younger on the last deal.

Notes on procedure. It must be understood that Piquet is by nature an 'open' game, and not governed by the many rules of secrecy that surround others. We have noted, for example, that no card or cards scored in a combination may remain unidentified: if it is not obvious from one player's own hand exactly which cards constitute a combination for which his opponent scores, he is entitled to ask and must be truthfully answered. (This does not apply, however, to any card undeclared or 'sunk'. For example, if elder holds four Kings but only declares three, and is acknowledged good, younger may ask him which three he is counting – or which one he is not counting – and elder, obliged to give some reply, may announce whichever one he pleases to be 'not counted'. He is not obliged to declare that he has sunk anything.) During the play, each player may refer to his own discards whenever he likes, and may examine previous tricks won by both players. The opponent of a player who has scored for point may, at any time during the trick play, ask his opponent how many he has left of his point suit, and must be answered (if only to save time, since he can find out by examining the tricks).

If a player leads out of turn, his opponent may tell him to take the card back, and there is no penalty; but if his opponent follows to such a lead, the trick stands as good and there may be no correction. If one player revokes (fails to follow suit although able to do so), all cards played from the commission to the discovery are taken back into hand and play proceeds without penalty. To save time, a player holding a suit of unbeatable cards, such as A K T 9 8 7, may play them simultaneously, announcing 'from the top' and requiring the other to play an equal number of cards. The latter, however, should not do so unless he agrees that they automatically win. If not, he need play only to the winning cards, leaving those tricks to his opponent, and may then capture the highest remaining in order to take over the lead. Either player, believing himself to hold all losing cards, may throw his hand in to cede the remaining tricks, but may not then take any back upon discovery of a miscalculation. If one player lays the whole of his remaining cards on the table, being of more than one suit, and claims to win the balance of tricks, his opponent must then either (a) concede, or (b) show that there is at least one losing card amongst them, in which case he himself is deemed to win the whole of the balance. The purpose of this rule, of course, is to prevent one player from discovering whether or not his opponent has made a certain losing discard and profiting from the discovery.

If either player is discovered to hold more cards than he is entitled to, his penalty is to score nothing for that deal. But any combination held good prevents his opponent from scoring in that class, or from scoring pique or repique, and any trick he takes guards him against the capot. It is up to each player to ensure that he has the right number, as there is no compensation (or penalty) for holding too few. In the latter event, tricks to which he cannot play score to his opponent. A misdeal may be corrected without penalty if discovered before either player has taken his cards into hand. If a card is faced in the deal or found faced in the pack, the same player deals again.

If elder announces a combination lower in value than the best he holds, and younger replies 'not good', he may not revise his call but must leave younger to score in that class.

Illustrative deal

The following example, borrowed from the standard work by Cavendish,[5] is provided for no other purpose than to clarify the basic rules of procedure. The only alteration I have made is to change the players from 'A' and 'B' to 'Napoleon' and

5. Cavendish, *Piquet* – 6th Edition (LONDON, 1889).

'Josephine'. Josephine deals, making Napoleon elder hand, and the cards are:

Nap: ♠A K J ♡A Q J 8 ♣J 8 7 ♢9 8
Jos: ♠T 7 ♡T 9 7 ♣K Q T ♢A Q J T

Napoleon has up to five exchanges, and hopes to draw more hearts and the 'fourteenth' Jack. He therefore discards ♠K and the two low clubs and diamonds.

Josephine must keep her fourteen Tens and discards ♠7 ♡9 ♡7. After the draw, the hands are:

Nap: ♠A J 9 8 ♡A K Q J 8 ♣J 9 ♢K
Jos: ♠Q T ♡T ♣A K Q T ♢A Q J T 7

Declarations proceed as follows:

Nap Point of five.
Jos (*also having a point of five*) Worth?
Nap 49.
Jos (*with 48*) Good.
Nap In hearts. And a quart major. (*Meaning a sequence of four to the Ace.*)
Jos Good.
Nap That's five for point, four for the sequence nine ... (*Looks for another sequence to count, but fails to find any. His next call is somewhat tentative.*) Three Jacks?
Jos Not good.
Nap (*leading ♡A*) And one's ten.
Jos I count fourteen Tens and three Queens, seventeen.

Tricks are played as follows, each announcing their score upon winning a trick.

Nap	*Jos*		
♡*A*	♡T	(1)	*Nap* Eleven.
♡*K*	♢7	(1)	*Nap* (*playing all his hearts simultaneously*) Twelve, thirteen, fourteen, fifteen.
♡*Q*	♢T	(1)	
♡*J*	♢J	(1)	
♡*8*	♢Q	(1)	*Jos* (*repeating her score*) Seventeen.

◇K	◇*A*	(2)	
♣9	♣*A*	(1)	*Jos* Nineteen. (*Lays out all her clubs*)
♣J	♣*K*	(1)	Twenty, twenty one, twenty two,
♠8	♣*Q*	(1)	twenty three
♠9	♣*T*	(1)	
♠*A*	♠Q	(2)	*Nap* Seventeen.
♠*J*	♠T	(1)	*Nap* Eighteen, and ten for cards twenty eight.
			Jos Twenty three.

If this hand is played over it will be found that Napoleon would only have divided the cards, failing to score ten for the majority, if he had led spades after his run of hearts. As it is he just comes out ahead of Josephine with an average elder score of 28, whereas Josephine has more than younger usually expects to score and will hope to push ahead as elder on the next deal.

Suggestions for play

The difference in strategy as between dealer and non-dealer is more marked in Piquet than in any other two-hand game save perhaps Cribbage. Elder (non-dealer) starts with all the advantages, being entitled to five of the eight cards of the stock, having the lead and so determining the point of attack, and being alone able to score for pique. Younger's draw of usually only three cards is rarely sufficient to rescue a bad hand from disaster, while only he can find himself in the position of holding all eight cards of a suit and yet lose every trick. As if further proof were needed, statistics show that elder scores nearly twice as much as younger, on average. It follows that elder is in a position to take chances and should play an attacking hand, while younger should see to his defence first and not take chances that might weaken them.

To start, then, elder should always seek to exchange his full entitlement of five cards, for to take fewer is to waste his overwhelming advantage and to give younger considerably more room to manoeuvre. If he takes only four cards instead of five, he has reduced his advantage by 20 per cent but increased younger's by 33 per cent. Cards taken in excess of those he feels necessary to his hand are not wasted, as they are not only denied to younger but also remain unknown to him.

As elder hand, which five cards should you throw out? This is a problem that beginners find hard to solve, as they tend to feel that only non-combinable and non-trick-winning Nines, Eights and Sevens should be discarded, and if they have only three or four such cards will prefer to take less than their entitlement. What you should do, however, is to look at it the other way: decide which cards you must retain for the best chances of combining, and throw out the rest.

Of those to retain, the most important are usually those of your potential point – the suit of which you hold the greatest number of cards, or, if equal, that with the highest pip-values or best chances of turning into a sequence. The point in this hand, for example, is hearts:

♠AKJT ♡QJT9 ♣AQ ◇K9

since either of two cards (King or Eight) will convert it to a quint, which is twice as many chances as the solitary Queen that will make a quint in spades. The quint is particularly worth going for as it would be 'good against the cards' – meaning that it is obvious from your own cards that younger could not possibly draw an equal or better sequence. The discards from this hand, therefore, are ♠J ♠T ♣Q ◇K ◇9.

Discards are also made with a view to completing a quatorze, and problems can arise because this combination tends to cut across the discard requirements relevant to point or sequence. The hand above was not complicated by this factor because it contained two each of the valid ranks, thus ensuring that younger cannot score so much as a trio, but not offering strong enough chances of filling a quatorze to allow this hope to influence the discards. Furthermore, the potential quint would have been, if realised, good against the cards. But this superficially similar hand is far from easy:

♠AKJT ♡JT98 ♣AK7 ◇K

Again, there are virtually twice as many chances of making a quint or better in hearts (5 to 4 against, or 44%) as a quint in spades (3 to 1 against, or 25%). This time, however, it is not good against the cards, as younger might fill, or even have been dealt, an equal or better sequence in diamonds. Furthermore, you have three Kings and would prefer to keep them with a view to drawing the fourth, especially as younger may wind up with fourteen Queens. Since it is vital to restrict younger's entitlement to not more than three cards, you are faced with two possible ways of discarding from this hand.

1. Keep the heart sequence and the Kings, neither of which is at present good against the cards, and discard ♠A ♠J ♠T ♣A ♣7.
2. Keep the Kings and the potential spade quint, discarding the hearts and bottom club and drawing to ♠A K J T ♣A K ◇K.

(A third possibility is to forget the Kings and keep both spades and hearts in the hope of making two quints and repique, but the chances of doing so are too remote since only four cards can be exchanged.)

The chances of drawing the fourteenth King are the same in both cases. In case (1) there is a 1 in 4 chance of making the quint, and in case (2) there are 4 in 9. But although the latter gives better odds, it would lose if younger had a sixieme in diamonds and might tie if he has a quint, whereas the quint major (to the Ace) in the former would be good against a diamond quint. Further, if younger gets only five diamonds instead of six, the retention of spades here stands a better chance of scoring for point because the cards held are higher in value (as it stands, worth 31 against only 27). On the whole, then, case (2) is the safer holding against younger's possibilities, even though case (1) gives better chances on the face of it.

To summarise, elder should nearly always exchange up to his maximum of five cards, unless the hand dealt is so strong as to contain a quint or quatorze and the chance of (re)pique or capot. The longest suit should be kept intact for point, or, if suits are of equal lengths, then that with the highest count or longest sequence should be retained. A trio should be kept intact with a view to the quatorze, except that a trio of Tens or Jacks may be broken if the cards show that younger may hold a higher ranking quatorze and there are other pressures for discarding from them. If it becomes essential to choose between keeping the point or the trio, go for the point. Having classified cards into those that must be kept for combinations and those that need not, prefer to discard unneeded Aces and Kings rather than discard fewer than five, unless this spoils the chance of capot. If discarding requires it, do not hesitate to unguard Kings or Queens. Discard from as few different suits as possible. Unless it contains a card needed for a combination, it is often as well to throw out the whole of a suit as part of it, and sometimes even better.

As younger hand, your approach is quite different. Having normally only three cards to exchange, you have considerably less opportunity to draw to high combinations. The question of tricks is also of greater importance, since – to take an extreme case – you can be capoted though holding a handful of high cards, if they are of suits in which elder is void. Whereas elder can usually expect to win the cards (take more tricks) with an average hand and proper play, younger must usually discard and fight to at least divide them (six each).

Your first concern, then, after looking for carte blanche, is to ensure adequate coverage in all suits to avoid the danger of capot. A hand such as this;

♠AKJ987 ♡JT9 ♣Q9 ◇8

will lose every trick if elder, as is likely, has no spade in hand. Here it is vital, before thinking about combinations, to cover the three weak suits by discarding spades. Even the lowly ◇8 must be retained, to act as a guard in case the King is drawn. Of course, the probability of drawing one guard in each of the three suits is extremely low, but at least two should be drawn to defend against capot. Even then, it may be hard to find the right discards to elder's winning leads. Quite apart from tricks, the potential combinations are not worth much. From the cards, there is every chance that elder will hold seven diamonds, and even six clubs would be worth more than your six spades. (Assess this quickly by noting that your spade suit lacks cards worth 20 in combined face value, whereas his six clubs would lack only 19, *ie* the Q+9 held by yourself.) And if you drew ♠Q for a quart major, he is likely to hold at least a quint in diamonds.

This hand, however, is an extreme case of weakness for tricks, and is introduced only to point out that a good-looking hand at first sight must be looked at very closely before any discarding decisions are made. As far as combinations are concerned, judge your discards in much the same way as for elder hand. Two points must be noted, though. First, do not aim for a particular combination if it means unguarding a suit or losing a vital trick. And second, although it is best for elder to exchange his full entitlement of five cards, as younger you should not hesitate to take only two or even one if it means throwing good cards after bad. In this case (unlike elder's situations) any cards you leave remain out of play instead of going into your opponent's hand.

To summarise: as younger, discard defensively with a view to retaining coverage in sufficient suits to avoid capot. Do not take all cards available if this means throwing out guards or trick-winners, and do not waste good cards in going after high combinations which are not good against the cards. Other things being equal, always keep your point suit, as it is your best and cheapest defence against pique/repique.

The next important part of the game is not the playing of tricks but the announcement of combinations. Practised players often enter the play with a pretty shrewd idea of their opponent's holding, gleaned from what he has announced in declarations together with an estimate of which of the other cards are more likely to be out of his hand than in it. For this reason it is important not to say more about your holding than you really need in order to establish whether or not your declaration is 'good'. Suppose, as elder, you hold:

♠Q J T 9 ♡A Q J T ♣A K T ◇T

You call a point of four; younger asks its value, and replies 'not good' to your 40. Your next declaration is fourteen Tens', with not a word about the sequence. Why? Because if your point of four is not good at 40, younger must have a point of four worth 41, and from your own holding you can see this to be ♢A K Q J. Your sequence of four is bound to be not good, so to mention it at all would only be to give him gratuitous information about your hand. Again, if as elder you held fourteen Kings after exchanging five cards, but had not seen hair nor hide of an Ace, there would be no point in announcing them unless younger took fewer than three cards, as he would certainly not have thrown an Ace with Kings against him. Similar considerations apply to younger. Suppose you hold:

♠A Q J T 7 ♡8 7 ♣Q J T ♢K 9

Your discards were two diamonds and a club. Elder calls a point of five. Without hesitation, you should immediately announce 'good'. Since his point can only be in hearts, it must be worth at least 49 to your 48 in spades, and there is no point in giving away free information.

It is because so many of the opposing cards are known by the time tricks are played that it has been said, in reference to this part of the game, that 'in Piquet, there are no surprises' – which is not quite true, but worth bearing in mind. Elder should normally lead his point suit from the top down, unless headed by a tenace (A–Q or, more especially, K–J); younger, when no longer able to follow, will start discarding from the bottom of his point, unless he is confident of gaining the lead and winning tricks with the whole of his point. A time for elder not to lead his point is when it lacks the top card and there is pique to be made by leading non-point winner – for example, from

♠K Q J T 8 ♡A K Q ♣A K ♢K Q

elder has point equal, a quart good plus tierce major making 7, fourteen Kings 21 and a trio of Queens 24, plus 1 for leading 25. He leads hearts and clubs, reaching 30 in tricks and adding 30 for pique. In defending against elder's point lead, younger must do everything to avoid unguarding suits, even to the extent of throwing out winners from his own point. For example:

♠Q8 ♡QJ9 ♣K7 ♢AKJT8

Elder, having counted point six and three Aces, leads his six spades. Younger must throw diamonds from the bottom up after playing his two spades, for if his sixth card is a heart or club he may well be capoted. If possible, of course, younger should keep his point and throw low cards from other suits if this can be done without losing the guard.

The addition of the rubicon has added much interest and excitement to the strategy of the game by sometimes making it vital to play to the score. If your opponent is well in the lead by the sixth deal, while you are still short of the rubicon, you are faced with a nice problem: whether to go all out to reach it, taking chances and playing boldly if need be, or, instead, to go for as few points as possible, by seeking equalities in combinations and playing to divide the cards. (If you are rubiconed, remember, your opponent adds your own score to his, plus 100 for game.)

If elder is trailing at the last deal and feels unable to reach 100, he will do best to sink everything he holds, even if (*especially* if!) this includes a quint or quatorze – in other words, declare nothing and let younger count whatever he holds as 'good'. There is no point in trying to equalise. As elder, you may be convinced that younger has point five and quint major as well as yourself, but if you declare either of them, younger will simply announce 'good' and let you make the score, since it will ultimately be credited to his own account. In trying to divide the cards, elder must not allow younger to manoeuvre him into taking the majority by 'suicide' play to tricks. Younger does not mind who wins the cards, so long as they are not divided.

If the positions are reversed, younger is somewhat better placed for declaring equalities, since elder has to announce first, and younger can sink as much as may be necessary to equalise. For example, suppose you hold a point consisting of K–Q–J–T–7, worth 47. Elder declares a point of four. You ask its value; he replies 'thirty nine'. You announce 'equal', sinking nine from your face value, and neither scores. Elder next announces a tierce to the Queen. Again, you equalise. By sinking the King, you also have a tierce to the Queen.

(Some players only allow whole cards to be sunk, thus making it illegal to sink nine from K-Q-J-T-7 since that value does not correspond to a card held. This nice point, not covered by the Portland Club Laws, should perhaps be agreed beforehand.)

It is easy to see the value of sinking for the purpose of keeping one's score low when certain of being rubiconed, but there are other circumstances in which advantage may be gained from it, or, indeed, when all depends upon it. Here is an extreme example, provided by Cavendish – who pointedly adds 'It is useless to practise this stratagem against an indifferent player who does not count your hand'. In other words, you can't bluff a fool. Elder holds:

♠AKQJ987 ♡K ♣AK ♢AK

After equalising on point (younger having seven hearts), elder is in a position to call fourteen Kings. But this would give his hand away. If younger knows he has the singleton ♡K, he will play everything except his red Ace and be assured of taking at least one trick. Elder therefore sinks his red King, knowing his trio of Aces and Kings to be good against the cards, because he himself discarded a Ten and can see that younger cannot hold a quatorze. Younger asks him which King he does not count, and elder (of course) replies 'hearts', which younger may believe or not, as he wishes. This puts younger in the unenviable position of choosing whether to throw all his hearts to elder's lead of spades in order to retain a guard in clubs or diamonds, or to hold back ♡A until the last trick in case elder has not discarded the King. By sinking, elder drops 11 points (counting 3 instead of 14 for Kings); against this, however, he has a good chance of making capot – except, as Cavendish says, 'against a very acute or very stupid player'. There are, of course, circumstances in which, as younger, one would sink an unguarded King in order to avoid being capoted.

Illustrative game

Only the sixth deal of the following illustrative game consists of deliberately concocted hands. The others I dealt normally from a properly shuffled pack specifically for the purpose of these illustrations, which may therefore be regarded as fairly representative. The comments on play may be regarded as those of an impartial observer.

First deal. Josephine cuts the higher card and elects to deal first. Quoting elder hand first, the cards fall thus:

Nap: ♠J ♡AKQJ8 ♣Q7 ◇QJ87
Jos: ♠987 ♡T97 ♣K9 ◇AKT9

Napoleon is faced with the interesting possibility of going for two quatorzes (Jacks and Queens) instead of pressing his point in hearts. But sets are counted last, so even if he were successful he would be unlikely to convert the 28 points into a repique. He therefore keeps his point and the three Queens, making exactly five discards.

Josephine has an unpleasant hand, being unguarded in two suits and holding a point in diamonds that is unlikely to convert into a sequence. In spades and hearts she can keep one and two cards to act as guards against the possible draw of nothing better than a King and a Queen, and accordingly throws ♠8 ♠7 ♡7.

After the draw, the new hands are:

Nap: ♠AQT ♡AKQJ8 ♣QJT ◇Q
Jos: ♠K9 ♡T9 ♣AK98 ◇AKT9

As luck would have it, Napoleon has not improved his point and would have made both quatorzes, giving him a score of 100 on declarations alone. Neither has Josephine improved her diamond point, but she has drawn a King in spades and is glad to have kept a guard for him. She can see five tricks in hand and will hope to be able to divide the cards.

Napoleon counts 5 for point, 4 and 3 for sequences, and 14 Queens for a total of 26. He leads ♡A for 1, then plays the rest of his hearts for 5 trick points. This brings him to 32, plus 30 for pique 62, since Josephine has not yet scored. To these leads she has played two hearts, two clubs and one diamond, from the lowest upwards.

If Napoleon now leads his ♠A he will only divide the cards. Holding a tenace in that suit himself, he must force Josephine to lead into it to give him the extra trick he needs to win 10 for the cards. He knows that she cannot hold more than two clubs and three diamonds, and must therefore stick at five tricks. Accordingly, he leads ♣Q. Josephine wins five tricks for 6, leads a spade, and Napoleon takes the last two for 3. With 10 for cards, Napoleon finishes with a score of 75 to Josephine's 6.

Second deal. Now Napoleon deals and the cards are as follows (elder hand first):

Jos: ♠A K J 7 ♡A K 7 ♣A J 9 8 ◇9
Nap: ♡Q J T 9 8 ♣Q T 7 ◇A T 8 7 (*no spades*)

Elder chooses spades for point, as it is not only worth more but also stands to convert to a better sequence. She must take in an Ace or Queen (or two Kings) to prevent Napoleon from counting a possible 14 Queens. Her discards are, clearly, a heart, a diamond, and the three bottom clubs.

Napoleon's discards are equally obvious. He must keep his point and quint in case he draws a spade with which to beat the elder hand, and must retain his guarded Queen in clubs. Out go the three low diamonds. After the draw:

Jos: ♠A K J T 9 8 7 ♡A K ♣A K ◇K
Nap: ♠Q ♡Q J T 9 8 ♣Q T 7 ◇A Q J

Josephine has not only succeeded in taking the fourth King to beat younger's queenly quatorze, but also wound up with a hand that is almost identical with Cavendish's illustration (p 62) of when to sink a King. This puts Jo in a quandary – shall she follow Cavendish's example, declare only three Kings, and hope thereby to lull Napoleon into believing her void in diamonds so that he will throw his diamonds away and let her win capot? No. For one thing, she has never heard of Cavendish, having flourished a good half century before him. For another, she knows her opponent well enough to know that he will hold back his ♢A as a matter of course. After all, he has seen six of the eight diamonds, and will not expect the other two to lie in elder's discards.

Battle commences. Josephine declares a point of seven, good, a quint to the Jack, not good, fourteen Kings and three Aces. Plus one for leading ♠A, and a score of 25. Napoleon declares a quint to the Queen for 15. Josephine takes her eleven tricks for 11, plus 10 for more and a total of 46. Napoleon's score is 15 for the quint plus one trick for 2, making 17. Combined totals to date: Napoleon 92, Josephine 51.

In retrospect, Josephine might have had second thoughts about sinking a King. She made the decision not to on the expectation of a good quint and consequent pique. Finding Napoleon with a better quint she might well have sought capot as a consolation.

Third deal. Josephine deals as follows:

Nap: ♠J 8 7 ♡K Q T 9 7 ♣K Q ♢K Q
Jos: ♠K T ♡J 8 ♣A T 8 7 ♢J T 9 7

Not an easy one for elder, with only three obvious discards. He must either spoil his point and go for two quatorzes (not good against the cards unless he also draws an Ace), or split Kings or Queens, or discard only three. He decides to throw out two Queens.

Josephine's hand is no easier, with only two suits guarded and mediocre chances of a good point or sequence. Preferring to keep the tierce in diamonds, she eventually throws out the three low clubs.

Nap: ♠A Q ♡A K Q T 9 7 ♣K 9 ♢K 8
Jos: ♠K T 9 ♡J 8 ♣A J ♢A J T 9 7

Having thrown out Queens, Napoleon naturally picks up the fourth Queen and two Aces, plus a guard to each King – which he does not really need, having a certain seven tricks. Younger has raised her point of four to five, but it will not be good, and she can see little hope of dividing the cards. A mediocre result all round. Napoleon counts a point of six, good, tierce major in his point suit, good, and three good Kings, total 12, and one for leading, 13. Josephine has nothing to declare.

Napoleon plays his hearts for 6, to which Josephine throws two hearts, a spade and three clubs (the lowest ranks first, of course). If he now plays his Ace for a seventh trick, she will take five tricks for 6. Instead, wishing to keep her score as low as possible with a view to the rubicon (she being only half way there), Napoleon boxes clever with ♣9. She takes it for 2 and returns ♢J. He takes it for 2 and returns ♣K. She takes it for 2 and cashes her ♢A for a fifth trick point – her last, since she must now lead into Napoleon's spade tenace, giving him two tricks for 3 plus 10 for the cards. Total on this deal: Napoleon 34, Josephine 5. Cumulative total half way through the game: Napoleon 126 and well over the rubicon, Josephine 56 and not yet in sight of it.

Fourth deal. Napoleon deals:

Jos: ♠K Q J 9 ♡Q 8 ♣A K 7 ♢A K J
Nap: ♠A 8 7 ♡A K 9 ♣J 9 ♢Q T 8 7

As elder, Josephine must keep her point in spades and hope to convert her trio of Kings into a quatorze. As it stands, the trio is not good against the cards, as younger may hold or acquire '14 Tens'. To prevent this, she must find a fifth discard. Rather than spoil her point, she drops an Ace, throwing out ♡Q ♡8 ♣7 ♢A ♢J. (Why not the Ace of clubs ? A fine point – almost a matter of principle rather than practicality. Her diamond suit is marginally stronger than her clubs, therefore his club suit may be marginally stronger than his diamonds, so she had better keep her strength in clubs.)

Napoleon's younger hand is hardly problematical, nor hardly promising either. He keeps his point suit, avoids breaking up clubs in case the Queen appears, and so discards two low spades and the bottom heart. Now:

Jos: ♠K Q J T 9 ♡T 7 ♣A K T 8 ♢K
Nap: ♠A ♡A K J ♣Q J 9 ♢Q T 9 8 7

Josephine announces 'five', to which Napoleon replies 'good' immediately, knowing that his diamond point is weaker and not wishing to reveal its length. Josephine adds '. . . in spades, and a quint to the King adds 15', (knowing it to be good against the cards) '20; three Kings 23 and Tens 26; one for leading 27'.

It will be noted that Josephine's trios were also good against the cards, and that her failure to announce three Aces tells Napoleon that she has discarded one – whether it tells him truthfully or not is for him to decide, but there would seem little point in bluffing.

Within three points of pique, Josephine secures the bonus by leading her two top clubs and ♢K, the latter winning because she discarded the Ace. Napoleon played his Jack and Nine of clubs and Jack of hearts, leaving himself with top cards in all suits by the time Jo has announced her score as 60. Whatever she leads next, Napoleon takes nine for 10 plus 10 for the cards, 20 in all. Scores at end of fourth deal: Napoleon 146, Josephine 116 and now over the rubicon.

Fifth deal. Josephine deals:

Nap: ♠Q J T 7 ♡A 7 ♣A K 9 ♢A 9 8
Jos: ♠A K 9 8 ♡Q T 9 ♣J 7 ♢Q J 7

Napoleon has only four obvious discards after keeping his spade point and all Aces and Kings. Should he just exchange four, or spoil his point by throwing the Seven, or throw out ♣K as the fifth card? He decides to dispense with ♠7, which is exactly what I would have done.

Josephine's younger hand is, if possible, even more unpromising. After little thought, out go the numeral spades and bottom club. The Queens must not be unguarded, for younger is often capoted with only one good suit in hand.

Nap: ♠Q J T ♡A J ♣A K Q T ♢A K T
Jos: ♠A K ♡K Q T 9 8 ♣J 8 ♢Q J 7

A typical quiet hand. Napoleon's point of four is not good, but he counts two tierces for 6, plus 6 for his trios of Ace and Ten, plus one for leading 13. Josephine counts 5 for her point in hearts.

In the play of tricks, elder must prevent younger from establishing hearts by forcing her to throw some of them to his leads. He kicks off in diamonds, hoping to find the Queen bare. Upon receipt of Josephine's Seven, however, he turns to his point in clubs. Younger, after following suit twice, can do neither better nor worse than to discard hearts from the bottom up. At this stage Napoleon cannot find any sure way of taking the last trick – which would give him the advantage of a measly point – so cashes his ♡A and ◇K, allowing Josephine to win the last five tricks for 6. To his opening 13, then, Napoleon has added a point each for seven won tricks, plus 10 for the cards, 30. Totals now, with the last deal coming up: Napoleon 176, Josephine 123.

Sixth deal. Trailing by 53 points, Josephine, as elder on the last hand, looks in need of at least a pique to win the game. The hands are:

Jos: ♠A T 9 ♡A T 7 ♣A 8 7 ◇T 9 7
Nap: ♠8 7 ♡J 9 8 ♣K Q J 9 ◇K Q J

Not a promising hand for elder on the last deal – no point suit and no sequences, though the trio of Aces may convert into a quatorze. Of immediate interest, however, is the absence of court cards, which at least gives her carte blanche for 10. 'I have a blank', she announces, 'and am going to exchange five cards. Make your discards before I show it.'

Now Napoleon must assess his hand. He knows the stock contains two Kings and Queens and a Jack. He must be very lucky indeed to take the fourth Jack *and* the Ace which might, if it is there, make those Jacks good against the cards. He discards both spades and the bottom heart.

Josephine now plays her cards rapidly face up to the table, counts 10 for the blank, and makes five discards – two diamonds, two clubs and the lowest heart. After the draw, the hands are:

Jos: ♠A K Q J T 9 ♡A T ♣A T ◇A T
Nap: ♡K Q J 9 ♣K Q J 9 ◇K Q J 8 (*no spades*)

As elder, Josephine calls a point of six, good, bringing her score to 16; a sixieme, good, 32, repique makes 92 (Napoleon having scored nothing); fourteen Aces and fourteen Tens, 120, plus 1 for leading, 121. With 9 for tricks and 10 for the cards, she reaches 140. Napoleon takes the last three tricks for 4.

The final result: Napoleon 180, Josephine 263. The difference is 83, and Josephine's game score, accordingly, 183.

This hand was deliberately concocted to show the highest score theoretically possible on one deal at Piquet. I say 'theoretically', because in order for it to be reached in practice younger would have to play with the aim of intentionally losing all the tricks. Thus, if Napoleon had suicidally played all his Kings and Queens to Josephine's spades, and then his Jacks to her Aces, she would have added to her original 121 a further 12 for tricks and 40 for capot – a grand total of 173.

The highest score which can be reached in practice is 170. It does not require younger to play stupidly, but does call – rather improbably – for elder's point of three to be 'good'. Holding A–K–Q in all suits, and finding all his combinations good, elder scores 3 for point, 12 for four tierces, 42 for three quatorzes, and repique for 60, total so far 117. One for leading makes 118, followed by 12 for tricks, 130, and capot, 170.

I raise this point because it is often said that the highest possible score on one hand of Piquet is 170. In fact, this is only the highest probable score, the highest *possible* being, as I have shown, 173.

8 BEZIQUE

A pretty and pleasing game affording much scope for tactical skill without overtaxing the intellect, Bézique may be particularly recommended as an accompaniment to the digestion of a splendid meal.

It is first cousin to the American game of Pinochle, and both appear to be descended from Sixty Six (described elsewhere in this book), or something very similar, via such intermediaries as Brusquembille, Briscan and Mariage – whence the terms *brisque* and *marriage* which figure prominently in the game.

The game was first played with a single 32-card pack, like Piquet, and known as Cinq Cents or Five Hundred, the winner being the first to reach that number. Early in the 19th century a two-pack, 64-card version seems to have sprung up in south-western France under the name Besi, which was transformed to Bésigue upon becoming a craze in the Paris gaming houses. This remains the French spelling to date.

A writer in Macmillans Magazine in 1861 sought to interest English players in the popular French game, but it did not really catch on until 1869 – possibly under the patronage of Victoria's son Alfred, Duke of Edinburgh, who picked it up in his travels and became addicted. (Eighty years later, Princess Margaret did much the same for Canasta.) The spelling of the name wavered for some time, only settling down with the discovery of Rubicon Bézique, which became something of a craze during Victoria's latter decades. Rubicon, played with four packs (128 cards), was succeeded by Chinese Bézique, using six, and ultimately by an even more elaborate eight-pack game requiring no fewer than 256 cards all shuffled together.

We will start with two-pack Bézique by way of introduction, and then, if you find this to your liking, proceed to higher things. The name *bézique* refers to the combination of ♠Q and ◇J in one hand, and may be connected with *besicle*, meaning 'spectacles, eye-glasses'. Similarly, Pinochle comes from *binocle*, which denotes the same combination and means the same thing. This may have arisen because in the commonest French pack the ♠Q and ♢J are the only Queen and Jack depicted in profile, thus exhibiting two eyes between them.

Two-pack Bézique

Equipment. Two 32-card packs shuffled together, consisting of A K Q J T 9 8 7 in each suit. It does not matter if they are of different back designs or colours, so long as they are of the same dimensions. Scores are made continually throughout the game, and can be kept on paper, though some sort of mechanical scorer is useful. Patent Bézique markers, of the same design as Whist and Piquet markers, are now antiques, but dial-type scorers are still produced from time to time. Even a Cribbage board will do. All Bézique scores are in tens, so twice round the crib board at 10 per hole gives a maximum of 1210 points, enough to be getting on with.

Rank. In each suit, cards rank: A T K Q J 9 8 7. Note the position of the Ten. It counts higher than King both in play and in cutting for the deal.

Deal. Whoever cuts the higher-ranking card may choose whether or not to deal first. Deal eight cards each in batches of three, then two, then three. Turn up the next card – the seventeenth – and lay it to one side between the two players. The suit of this card is the trump suit for the current deal and, if it is a seven, the dealer immediately scores 10 for it. Place the undealt cards face down across this card to form the stock, so that the turn-up projects from beneath it.

Object. The winner is the first player to reach 1000 points, which may take one or several deals. Points are scored for (a) capturing brisques (Aces and Tens) in tricks, counting 10 points each, and (b) through drawing and discarding, acquiring certain combinations of cards scoring anything from 20 to 500 points each.

Tricks. Non-dealer leads to the first trick. The second player need not follow suit, but may play any card he chooses. A trick is won with the higher card of the suit led, or the higher trump if any are played. If identical cards are played, the first beats the second. The winner of a trick lays the won cards before him (not necessarily face down), shows and scores for any scoring combination he may hold in his hand, then draws the top card of stock to restore his hand to eight. The trick-loser draws the next card of the stock, and the trick-winner then leads to the next trick. This continues until the stock is exhausted, when the rules of play change. The purpose of winning a trick may be to capture any brisque it contains, though brisques (Aces and Tens) are not actually counted into the score until the end of the hand, and do not add up to much. The main advantage of winning a trick is that only the winner may declare a scoring combination. The loser may hold one, but he can do nothing about it until he wins a trick.

Scoring combinations. Upon winning a trick, a player may declare and score for any one (not more) of the following combinations, by removing its constituent cards from his hand and laying them face up on the table before him. Such cards remain on the table, but continue to count as part of his hand – *ie*, in subsequent tricks, he may play either from the hand or from a combination-card on the table before him.

(*a*)	*Sequence* (A T K Q J of trumps)	250
(*b*)	*Royal marriage* (K–Q of trumps)	40
(*c*)	*Common marriage* (K–Q of plain suit)	20
(*d*)	*Hundred Aces* (any four Aces)	100
(*e*)	*Eighty Kings* (any four Kings)	80
(*f*)	*Sixty Queens* (any four Queens)	60
(*g*)	*Forty Jacks* (any four Jacks)	40
(*h*)	*Bézique* (♠Q–◇J)	40
(*i*)	*Double bézique* (♠Q–◇J–♠Q–◇J)	500

Special rules govern the formation and re-formation of such combinations. The basic principle is that a card which has already been used as part of a scoring combination (and is therefore still lying on the table) may be used again as part of a different type of combination, but not of the same. Cards won in tricks remain out of play and cannot be used to form combinations.

Examples of re-use: If a marriage has been declared in spades, three more Queens might be added on the next turn to score Sixty Queens, and ◇J on the turn after to score bézique, so long as the ♠Q remains on the table throughout and is not played to a trick. If a royal marriage is declared for 40, then so long as both cards remain on the table it is permissible to add A–T–J of trumps and score 250 for the sequence.

Restrictions on re-use: If a marriage has been declared in spades, neither card may be remarried by the addition of another King or Queen (but another spade marriage may be scored by declaring the other King *and* Queen). Once a quartet (of Aces, Kings, Queens or Jacks) has been declared, none of its cards may be added to form another quartet, though it is permissible (if improbable) to declare another four of a kind straight from the hand to the table. It is also not permitted to declare a sequence for 250 and subsequently claim the royal marriage contained within it – as shown above, you must score the lower first and then the higher. Similarly, it is not permissible to score 500 for double bézique and subsequently count each constituent bézique for 40, but it is correct to declare, while winning three tricks, single bézique once, single bézique twice, and then double bézique, so long as all four bézique cards are on the table when double is declared.

It is sometimes stated that a combination is scorable only if at least one of its cards is played directly from the hand. This is not so. For example, it is proper to declare Kings for 80, Queens for 60 at the next opportunity, and then, so long as the appropriate cards remain on the table, a marriage upon winning each of the next four tricks. Or suppose Kings have been declared for 80, and two have been played out, leaving ♡K ♠K on the table. At a later turn, it is permissible to play ♠Q–◇J from the hand and announce 'bézique for 40, and a marriage to score', subsequently counting the ♠K–♠Q upon winning another trick.

Seven of trumps. A player who holds a Seven of trumps may declare it at any time – usually upon playing it to a trick – and score 10 points for it. Alternatively, he may, upon winning a trick, declare it for 10 and exchange it for the turn-up. This, however, counts as a declaration, and prevents him from declaring any other combination at the same time. (There are conflicting rules on the use of the trump Seven. This one is a recommended compromise.)

End-game. When the loser of the 24th trick has taken the turn-up into his hand, and there are no more cards in stock, the rules of play change. Each takes into hand any cards he has left on the table, and the last trick-winner leads to the first of the last eight tricks. The second to a trick must follow suit if he can and must win the trick if he can. If unable to follow, he must trump if he can. No combinations may be declared during this part of the game. The winner of the last trick scores 10 points for it. (*Variants* (a) 10 is scored for winning the 24th trick instead of the 32nd, *ie* the last trick before the stock is exhausted instead of the last trick of all. (b) The last eight tricks may be played as at whist, with Ten ranking between Nine and Jack, and obligation to follow suit if possible but not necessarily to win the trick. Not recommended.)

Score. Each player sorts through his won cards, counting 10 points for each Ace and Ten captured. This total is then added to his total for combinations and the result recorded. As many more deals are played as are necessary, until at least one player has reached 1000 points, the winner being the player with the higher total. If the loser has failed to reach 500, the winner counts double the margin of victory.

Suggestions for play

It is generally not worth winning a trick unless it contains a brisque or you have something to declare. Indeed, other things being equal, it is preferable to lose a trick and play second to the next one, as this gives you more latitude – for example, you know whether or not you can safely win it with a brisque, whereas you will avoid leading one for fear of losing it. On the other hand, situations often arise in which you suspect that your opponent has a valuable declaration to make, in which case you may attempt to keep winning tricks until the stock is exhausted in order to prevent him from declaring it. Bearing in mind that the same will be done against you, try to keep back trumps, especially high ones, to ensure the ability to declare.

It is obvious that good cards to throw to worthless tricks, or lead to those in which you have no interest, are Sevens, Eights and Nines. Often, however, you find yourself with none in your hand, which seems to consist of part-combinations and valuable cards. In this case treat Jacks as dispensable, as Forty Jacks is not a very high scoring combination and not worth spoiling the hand for. Keep hold of a diamond Jack, however, so long as there is the possibility of making bézique. Also be prepared to play a Ten if you can win the trick by doing so, as Tens cannot form part of scoring combinations except in trumps and are therefore not worth keeping from this point of view.

When it comes to breaking up part-combinations, you must weigh the value of each against the probability of making it, to which end you will be guided by what you can see amongst your opponent's declarations and what has already been played to tricks. For example, if he has declared a marriage in spades and you hold both Jacks of diamonds, it is impossible to make double bézique, and so one more Jack becomes available for discarding – unless, of course, you have seen so few of the eight Jacks to date that there seems a fair chance of forming a Jack quartet.

Cards still lying on the table after being declared are suitable candidates for playing to tricks, on the principle that you give your opponent less information about the state of your hand by playing a card he knows you have rather than one he hasn't seen. Marriage partners and quartetted Jacks are particularly good candidates for this purpose. At the same time, however, it is important to retain those which stand a fair chance of being re-used in other combinations, and those which belong to the

STOCK

trump suit and may therefore be needed for trick-winning. In particular, never break up (by playing a card from) a single bézique so long as the possibility remains of forming a second and scoring the double, as double bézique is the most valuable combination in the pack and will nearly always win the game.

Given a choice of combinations, it is naturally better to score the more valuable ones first. But there is an exception to this rule, in that (a) given a sequence, you may score 40 for the royal marriage first and then 250 for the sequence for a total of 290, but if you count the higher combination first you are restricted to 250, as the marriage may not then be scored; and (b) the same applies to béziques: you may declare, on three successive turns, a single, a single and a double, for a total of 580, but cannot score for a single after counting the double. In these cases you score more for starting with the lower combination and working upwards. If, however, it seems unlikely that you will have time to make these scores the long way, in view of the number of tricks left to play and the state of your own hand, then it may be better to score the higher combination first and forgo the lower.

In the last eight tricks, the ideal is to play worthless cards of a suit in which your opponent is void, in order to weaken his

FIGURE 4

A situation in Two-pack Bézique. (Players' won tricks are omitted from view, for clarity.) North has evidently scored '100 Aces' earlier on and has since played one of them to a trick. The rules forbid him to add another Ace to those on the table to score the same again, though this is permissible in versions played with more cards. He has also scored either 20 for a marriage in spades, having played out the King, or 40 for single bézique, having played out the Jack. If he draws another Queen, he will be able to declare '60 Queens' by adding it and the Queens in his hand to that on the table. If he has just won a trick, he may exchange the ♢7 for the turned-up Jack of trumps (for 10) and subsequently add the Jack to either of his spade Queens for bézique. As it happens, South is also much in need of this Jack. He has already scored 40 for the royal marriage in diamonds. Any Jack will give him '40 Jacks' to score, and the ♢J in particular could be added to his table K–Q and hand A–T to score 250 for the trump sequence.

trumps. Experienced players will know what cards their opponent holds and play accordingly. Experience, in fact, is essential to success at Bézique, as it is a game of judgement rather than analysis. The practised player soon develops an instinctive feel for the state of his opponent's hand, and will know when he can safely lose tricks and when he must keep winning to prevent a high combination from being scored against him.

Polish Bézique

Also known as Fildinski, Polish Bézique differs from the ordinary game in only one major respect – yet the difference is so great as to produce a game of quite different feel, and one that many Bézique players prefer to the main game, finding it more demanding of skill. Certainly one has more control over the cards, and less depends on the luck of the draw.

Polish Bézique is played either with two 32-card packs (64 cards) up to 2000 points, or with three packs (96 cards) up to 3000. The following features are exactly the same as at Bézique: numbers of cards dealt, establishment of trump suit, exchange or declaration of Seven of trumps, method of playing tricks, need to win a trick before declaring, value of brisques and of scoring combinations.

The difference is that declarations can only be made of cards won in tricks. A card may not be played from the hand to the table to form a combination. Upon winning a trick, a player discards Nines, Eights and Sevens as worthless (apart from scoring 10 for the trump Seven, and exchanging it if desired), scores 10 for any brisque it contains, and lays the other cards face up on the table before him. If one or more combinations can be made with either or both of the cards just captured in the trick, they must be announced and scored before the next card is drawn from stock, otherwise they are lost. Cards used in combinations remain face up on the table, but may be played to tricks, and none may be used twice in a combination of the same type.

The play of the last eight tricks follows the same rules as Bézique (follow and head the trick if possible; trump if unable to follow), but combinations may still be declared from cards taken in tricks right up to the end of play. When played with three packs, triple bézique scores 1500.

Rubicon (Four-pack) Bézique

Also known as Japanese Bézique, for those who like artificial ethnic flavouring, Rubicon increases the fun of the game by doubling the number of cards, increasing the number of combinations, and lifting restrictions on re-forming them, with the result that extremely high scores are to be made. Following a similar principle to that of the rubicon in the game of Piquet, that of Rubicon Bézique is set at 1000 points. If the loser of the game fails to reach that total, he is heavily penalised, especially if he is foolish enough to play for money. In the following description, it is assumed that the reader is already acquainted with the basic two-pack game.

Cards. Four 32-card packs shuffled together very thoroughly.

Deal. Nine cards each, either one at a time or in batches of three. Place the remainder face down to form a stock. There is no turn-up.

Carte blanche. If either player has been dealt a hand containing not a single court card, he may claim carte blanche for 50 points by playing his cards rapidly, one at a time, face up to the table in order to prove it. He then takes them back into hand. If the next card he draws from stock during the course of play is also a blank, he may show it and score 50 again, and may do so for as often as he continues to draw a blank on subsequent turns. As soon as he draws a King, Queen or Jack, however, his privilege of scoring for carte blanche ceases for the rest of the deal.

Trumps. There is no trump suit to start with, and a trick can only be won by the higher card of the suit led, or the first played of identical cards. The first marriage declared scores 40, and the suit of that marriage takes immediate effect as the trump suit for the deal. (If a sequence is declared before a marriage, it also establishes trumps, but the royal marriage cannot then be scored separately.)

Tricks. Except that the game is played at no trump until a marriage is declared, the rules of trick-play are the same as at Two-pack Bézique, including the change of rule that obtains when the stock is exhausted and the last nine tricks are being played. It is customary for cards played to tricks to be left face up in the middle of the table until a brisque (Ace or Ten) is played, when the trick-winner gathers up all that have so far been played and stacks them on the table before him.

Briques. The score of 10 per won brisque is not counted until the end of the game, and even then is only used to break a tie. The game therefore depends mainly on scoring combinations.

Declarations. The winner of a trick may declare and score for one of the following combinations. These are basically the same as at Two-pack Bézique, but with the addition of a non-trump sequence and more multiple béziques.

SEQUENCES:		
(*a*)	*Trump sequence* (A T K Q J of trumps)	250
(*b*)	*Plain sequence* (A T K Q J of a non-trump suit)	150
(*c*)	*Royal marriage* (K–Q of trumps)	40
(*d*)	*Common marriage* (K–Q of non-trump suit)	20
QUARTETS:		
(*e*)	*Hundred Aces* (any four Aces)	100
(*f*)	*EightyKings* (any four Kings)	80
(*g*)	*SixtyQueens* (any four Queens)	60
(*h*)	*Forty Jacks* (any four Jacks)	40
BEZIQUES (♠Q– ◇J):		
(*i*)	*Quadruple bézique*	4500
(*j*)	*Triple bézique*	1500
(*k*)	*Double bézique*	500
(*l*)	*Single bézique*	40

As a point of difference from the two-pack game, there is no score for a Seven of trumps. A more startling difference is that a single card may be used more than once in the same type of combination, though not in an inferior combination of the same class.

Let us clarify the last point first. It is the same as before: a marriage may be scored first, and other cards subsequently added to score the sequence; but if a sequence is scored first, the marriage within it cannot be scored thereafter. Similarly, béziques may be scored one at a time for the single scores, then later declared as double, triple, and so on, for more; but once (say) triple bézique has been scored, its constituent béziques may not be scored separately thereafter.

Otherwise, the general rule is that as soon as a card has been played out of a combination and into a trick, it may be replaced by an equivalent card and the re-formed combination scored again. For example, if Kings have been declared for 80 and one of them is played to a trick, the quartet may be reconstituted and rescored by the addition of another King, either from the hand or from the table (e.g. forming part of a marriage), as soon as the holder wins another trick. As to béziques, note that a multiple bézique is only scorable if all its cards are visible simultaneously. But if, say, double bézique is on the table, and one of the Queens is played out, another ♠Q may subsequently be declared and the double bézique thereby scored again. Marriages are equally prolific, with partner-swapping allowable on a highly permissive scale. To take an extreme example, suppose four marriages have been declared in the same suit, and all eight cards are still on the table. On each one of his next six opportunities to declare, the holder may play one of these cards to a trick and score for another marriage so long as a King and Queen of the same suit remain. If a card is played from a sequence, it may be replaced on the next turn and the sequence scored again. Furthermore, although a marriage cannot be declared if it lies in a sequence that has been scored, it can be scored by the addition of a second King or Queen if the first is played to a trick, after which the sequence itself is scorable again. Clearly, it is a matter of some importance to keep track of which cards have already been used in the formation of additional marriages.

The only real restriction is that only one score may be made at a time, and that only upon winning a trick. If the addition of cards to the table creates several different combinations, it is desirable to score the highest and announce the others as being 'to score', and to repeat this until the opportunity arises to score them. For example, suppose you have double bézique on the table and then declare eighty Kings, two of them being spades. You announce 'Eighty Kings and two marriages to score'. You draw another King, play a King and win the trick. You are now not obliged to score the marriage, as you can first, more profitably, put the King down and again announce 'Eighty Kings and still two marriages to score' (or, if the King you played was a spade, 'and one marriage to score').

End-game. When the last card has been drawn from stock and the last declaration made, all cards are taken into hand and the last nine tricks played in the same way as the last eight at Two-pack Bézique. There is a bonus of 50 for winning the last trick.

Score. If both players have exactly the same score, brisques are counted in to break the tie, and if they fail to do so the game is drawn. Otherwise brisques are ignored, except to escape the rubicon as explained below. Each player rounds his final score down to the nearest hundred below, and the winner scores 500 plus the difference between the two rounded scores. But the loser is credited with 100 even if he made less, and if the scores round down to the same amount the higher score is rounded up instead.

The rubicon. Regardless of what the winner scored, the loser is rubiconed if he fails to make 1000 points, though if he has won enough brisques to bring his score to this level he may demand that both players count their brisques in and thereby escape the rubicon. If this fails, he does not count his brisques, and the winner scores all points made by both players, plus 1000 for game, plus 300 'for brisques'.

Settlement. This complicated scoring system was made with pecuniary settlement in mind, the game being played at so much per hundred points.

Notes on play. Basic principles of play at Four-pack Bézique are much the same as for the two-pack game, with three major exceptions. First, as we have already noted, the game is essentially one of combinations. As brisques are only counted in the event of ties or being otherwise rubiconed, there is less need to win tricks containing them, and Aces and Tens (especially Tens) are therefore more readily available for winning tricks. Coupled with this is the fact that the almost endless possibilities of combination and re-combination call for a greater degree of judgement – a sharper degree of observation of the possibilities available together with a more accurate assessment of which are worth pursuing and which can be dropped if necessary. The third point arises out of the method of determining trumps. It is often inadvisable to make trumps just because you can. If you are well represented in all suits, holding perhaps a marriage or two, it does not matter too much if your opponent makes trumps first. When you find one of your suits predominating, then is the time for trump-making, with a view to converting into a trump sequence. You may also be guided by what your opponent is discarding. If it is clear that he is keeping back a suit, apparently building it up for greater effect, you might well make trumps earlier in order to upset his plans.

Chinese (Six-pack) Bézique

The difference between what was originally devised as Chinese Bézique and what is now known as Six-pack Bézique is fairly subtle. I believe I'm right in stating that unadulterated Chinese Bézique was no more than Rubicon (Japanese) Bézique played with six packs instead of four, and that the 'Chinese' tag was dropped with the addition of certain 'optional extra' rules which will be carefully noted below so that you may decide beforehand whether to follow them or not. Six-pack really is the game for Bézique enthusiasts – amongst whom legend not only numbers the late Sir W S Churchill as a devotee but indeed also credits him with considerable expertise.

Cards. Six 32-card packs shuffled together, 192 cards in all, ranking as at other forms of Bézique.

Optional rule. The dealer (established by cutting, as usual) attempts in one movement to lift exactly 24 cards off the top of the pack, and the non-dealer announces his estimate of how many cards he thinks have in fact been lifted. If the dealer succeeds, he scores 250; if non-dealer's estimate is right, he scores 150. It is, of course, possible for both to score if non-dealer correctly guesses twenty-four. (This optional rule has been criticised as having nothing to do with the game. I do not concur. For one thing it is fun, and for another it strikes me as a more valid exercise of 'skill at cards' than the mere application of memory, for which many existing games give too high rewards.)

Deal. Twelve cards each, one at a time. Place the remainder face down to form a stock.

Carte blanche. As at Rubicon Bézique, but scores 250 each time.

Play. As at Rubicon Bézique, with trumps established by the first marriage (or sequence) declared, and with the following additional scoring features:

Four Aces of trumps	1000
Four Tens of trumps	900
Four Kings of trumps	800
Four Queens of trumps	600
Four Jacks of trumps	400

Other quartets score as at Rubicon, with no score for four Tens if not all trump. Béziques score as at Rubicon, with no extra credit for quintuple or sextuple. The last trick of all scores 250 to its winner. Brisques play no part at all.

Optional trump/bézique rules. Two rules are involved here, it being usual to play either both or neither. First, bézique is redefined as the Queen of trumps plus a Jack of opposite colour. If trumps are spades or diamonds, the Jack is diamonds or spades; if hearts or clubs, it is clubs or hearts. Second, if this rule is followed, the same suit may not be entrumped in two successive games. (This twin optional rule, never much favoured by English players, actually reduces rather than increases the variety of the game. Not recommended.)

Score. Each player's final total is rounded down to the nearest hundred, and the winner scores the difference plus 1000. If both round down to the same hundred, the higher-scoring player rounds up instead. If the loser fails to reach 3000 points he is rubiconed, and the winner scores 1000 plus the total of their two rounded scores (even if he fails to reach 3000 himself). If the final scores are identical the game is a draw – though it is easy, if desired, to devise tie-breakers. For example, (a) credit a final game score of 1000 to the winner of the last trick, or (b) play another game and credit its winner with an additional 1000 for game.

Notes on play. The additional hefty scores for trump quartets – including four trump Tens – may exert considerable bearing on your trump-making plans. Dealt three Aces of the same suit, for example, you will want to go all out to entrump that suit at the earliest opportunity. Without an obvious candidate, however, the decision when and what to make trumps is a matter of judgement born of experience. Much also depends on which rule you follow with regard to béziques. If sticking to the ♠Q–◇J definition regardless of trumps, for example, you may have to decide beforehand whether to go for multiple béziques or for trump sequences and quartets, a dichotomy that does not arise when the bézique Queen is always of the trump suit. In this connection, a reason for preferring the strict ♠–◇ definition of bézique is that games take on a quite different flavour according to whether trumps are spades, diamonds, or neither. Thus if your opponent appears to be collecting béziques, so far as you can tell from the failure of appropriate cards to fall into your own hands, or to be played to tricks by himself, you are in a good position to declare hearts or clubs as trumps. This will make his hand crowded, as he will have difficulty in collecting bézique cards while ensuring adequate coverage in trumps. A bézique suit as trump makes for a more economic hand.

The management of trumps requires some care. Don't bother to keep back small ones for the sake of hoarding, but at the other extreme do keep back trump Aces for maximum effect, both in the winning of tricks – especially towards the end and with a view to the last twelve – and for the possible acquisition (and re-formation) of a trump Ace quartet. But avoid crippling your hand for the sake of trump Tens, as they have no other value. It is better to aim for trump King or Queen quartets, as they can be milked for eighties and sixties while you wait for the appearance of the profitable fourth trump.

For the last twelve tricks it is desirable to retain not only trumps but also a long side suit with which to force the adverse hand. The point at issue is not to make brisques (they don't count) but to win the last trick. It will usually be taken by the better player – partly because he will have kept back better cards, partly because he will have kept closer track of the game and will know his opponent's entire hand, and partly because there is a marked element of skill in making the right moves in the right order, a point at which Bridge, Piquet and Pinochle players will excel. The last trick, at 250, is worth a twelfth of a rubicon and can make a substantial difference to the final game score.

Always keep an eye on both scores throughout the game – partly to check up on accurate score-keeping, but mainly to assess the chances of either player's being rubiconed. If you are in a winning position, be prepared to forgo combinations for the sake of preventing him from declaring enough to get him over the rubicon. If you can see no hope of escaping the rubicon yourself, remember that all scores made by both players will wind up in the winner's account, so win tricks to prevent him from declaring, but avoid declaring yourself. However, follow this course of action only if you are certain that the situation is desperate.

Eight-pack Bézique

This variant differs from Chinese Bézique only in the following particulars:

Cards. Eight 32-card packs, 256 in all.

Deal. Fifteen each.

Scoring combinations. In addition to those of the six-pack game there is quintuple bézique at 9000 points, while five trump Aces, Tens, Kings, Queens and Jacks score respectively 2000, 1800, 1600, 1200 and 800.

Score. As for the six-pack game, except that the rubicon is set at 5000 points.

One-pack Bézique (Binocle)

In case you have only a single pack, and wish to savour the delights of Bézique without rushing out to buy a second, there are several closely related games played with just 32 cards, including Binocle (Swiss), Binokel (German), Cinq Cents (French) and Marjolet (Spanish-French).

Binocle is played like ordinary (two-pack) Bézique, but with these differences:

1. No trump card is turned. Instead, the game is played at no trump until a marriage is declared, which establishes the trump for the rest of the hand.
2. The ♠Q–◇J combination is called binocle and scores 40.
3. The combination of ♠K–♠Q–◇J is called grand binocle and scores 80.
4. A sequence in trumps counts 150, not 250.
5. Instead of counting brisques at 10 each, certain cards captured in tricks bear point-values as follows: each Ace 11, Ten 10,

King 4, Queen 3, Jack 2. These may be scored as they occur or counted in at the end of play, whichever is more convenient.

6. Game is 500 points.

This game will be found to be remarkably similar to Sixty Six, to which we will turn next. English readers may also like to note that the American game of Pinochle, as played by two, is virtually Bézique but played with only 48 cards, all Sevens and Eights being removed.

9 SIXTY SIX

This popular German game goes back a long way and is an ancestor of the Bézique/Pinochle family. Though played with only 24 cards – even 20, in one variant – it is remarkably varied and exciting, and gives ample scope for skill. It may be characterised as a fast little game, suitable for play when time is limited or interruptions expected. Why it is not better known in Britain is a mystery, as similar games are quite widespread in Europe.

Sixty Six is said to have been invented in 1652 at an inn in Paderborn (North Rhine/Westphalia) called 'Am Eckkamp 66', and to have achieved such notoriety as a gambling game as to have called forth rapid prohibitions on play from legal and ecclesiastical authorities. (It may be remarked in passing that if such prohibitions did not exist it would be necessary to invent them, as they are essential to the pedigree of any popular game.) The following rules accord with those promulgated by the Sixty Six Research Circle, based in Paderborn.

The game

Cards. Twenty four, consisting of A K Q J T 9 of each suit.

Deal. Whoever cuts the higher card deals first, and the turn to deal alternates thereafter. Deal six cards each in batches of two at a time. Turn up the next (13th) card to establish trumps and lay it face up to one side. Place the undealt cards face down across it to form a stock in such a way that the trump card projects visibly beneath it.

Rank and value. Cards rank in the following order for trick-taking purposes (note the high position of the Ten) and bear a point-value credited to whoever wins them in a trick as follows:

Rank	A	T	K	Q	K	9
Value	11	10	4	3	2	0

Object. Each deal is won by the player who first scores 66 card points, for which he may score one, two or three game points. A game is won by the first to make seven game points, which will take at least three deals. Card points are scored for capturing counters (scoring-cards) in tricks, in accordance with the above table. As there are 30 card points in each suit and 10 points for winning the last trick, the total number of card points available is 130, of which the target number, 66, represents a clear majority. Additional card points are available for the declaration of marriages (each comprising a King and Queen of the same suit), as detailed below.

Tricks. Non-dealer leads to the first trick. The winner of each trick, before leading to the next, draws the top card of stock and adds it to his hand, and waits for his opponent to draw the next card. So long as any cards remain in stock, the rules of trick-play are as follows. The second to a trick need not follow suit but may play any card he pleases. The trick is won by the higher card of the suit led or by the higher trump if any are played. Won tricks are turned face down and may not be referred to. Each player must keep a mental record of the value of cards he has captured so far, it being illegal to record them in any other way.

Marriages. If a player holds the King and Queen of one suit, he may declare and score for the marriage only upon leading one of them to a trick. He must show both cards, and must have won at least one trick, in order to score the marriage. A marriage in trumps scores 40, in any other suit only 20.

Nine of trumps. The player holding the Nine of trumps may exchange it for the trump turn-up at any time, provided that he has won at least one trick, and that the turn-up has not yet been taken or turned down.

End of stock. When the last card of the stock (the trump turn-up or substituted Nine) has been drawn, the method of play changes. Marriages may no longer be declared. The follower to a trick must follow suit if he can and must win it if he can. If unable to follow, he must trump if he can. The winner of the last trick scores 10 for last.

Going out. As soon as a player has reached 66 or more card points, he may claim 'Out!', and play then ceases. If he is correct, he scores one game point, or two if his opponent is 'schneider' (*ie* has less than 33), or three if his opponent is 'schwarz' (has won no trick). If the caller is mistaken, his opponent scores two game points, increased to three if he has not taken any tricks. Note that the player who correctly calls 'Out' wins even if his opponent has taken more card-points, the latter being thereby penalised for failing to call when he could. Note, too, that the caller must already have taken 66 – he cannot count 10 for last if he ends the game prematurely.

If neither player calls, the cards are counted and the appropriate win (of one, two or three game points) goes to the player who has reached or exceeded 66. If both have reached 66, however, and neither has called, then the game point is held over and credited to the winner of the next deal, in addition to whatever score he makes for it in the usual way. If both players take exactly 65, the result is a draw and no game point is scored.

Closing. Either player, when it is his turn to lead to a trick, may close the stock by taking the trump turn-up and placing it face down on top of the remaining undrawn cards. The remaining tricks are then played out in exactly the same way as if the stock had run out naturally. The closer may, but need not, draw a sixth card before closing, so that the end-game may consist of five or six tricks. If he does draw, he must allow his opponent to do likewise. Furthermore, he must allow his opponent the opportunity of exchanging the Nine for the turn-up if so required. If the game is closed, there is no score of 10 for the last trick.

Variants

American Sixty Six. American practice differs in some details from the original game. In particular, marriages may still be declared in the play of the last tricks. One American source also notes that it is not necessary to head the trick in the end-game – that is, you must follow suit if possible, but are not obliged to play higher.

Mariage. This old French game (which explains why there is only one R in it) is virtually identical with Sixty Six. The chief point of interest is that a meld may be made consisting of the Ace and Ten of the same suit. This is called an *amour* and scores 30 in plain suits, 60 in trumps.

Illustrative deal

The players are Anton and Bernhard, of whom the latter deals as follows and turns ♣K for trumps:

Anton:	♣ *none* ◇K Q 9 ♠K ♡T K
Bernhard:	♣T ◇ *none* ♠Q J ♡Q J 9

In the following account, the card in brackets is the one drawn from stock after the trick has been taken.

Anton	Bernhard	
♡*K* (♠A)	♡9 (◇T)	As there is no obligation to follow suit, Bernhard would have done better to trump with his Ten. A has 4, B has 0.
◇Q (♠9)	◇*T* (♣J)	Having won a trick, Anton can now declare his diamond marriage for 20, duly leading one partner to the trick. Now A 24, B 13.
♠9 (♡A)	♣*J* (◇A)	B leads the only suit which A cannot capture with a high counter, except for the ♣A, which would leave B's Ten in a commanding position anyway. A 24. B 15.
◇9 (◇J)	◇*A* (♠T)	B takes a chance that A has no trumps, and is rewarded. A 24, B 26.
♠*A* (♣A)	♠J (♣Q)	A 37, B 26. After the draw, Bernhard, had he held ♣9, could have exchanged it for the turned trump King and made a royal marriage for 40. But now it is too late.
◇*J* (♣9)	♡J (♣K)	Anton has drawn ♣9 too late to exchange, and Bernhard, though he draws the King, cannot declare the

		marriage because the stock is exhausted. The score so far is A 41, B 26, and play is now governed by the strict rules of following to tricks.
♡*A*	♡Q	A 55, B 26.
♣*A*	♣Q	A 69, B 26. Anton now declares himself 'out', and scores not one but two game points because Bernhard is 'schneidered', having less than 33. (There is no '10 for last' because the last trick, which means the twelfth, was never played.)

Notes on play

Although using little basic material, Sixty Six is a game of surprising variety and almost pure skill. By half way through the game, when the stock is exhausted, each knows exactly what cards the other holds, and can calculate precisely how to play his own for the best. Even before this it is possible to make well-informed guesses as to the other's holding. For example, the *absence* of a marriage declaration from the other side indicates that a given King or Queen is yet to be drawn.

In the first part of the game it is essential, so far as possible, to retain marriages until they can be declared, and to save Aces and Tens for possible capture of adverse leads instead of leading them to risk loss by trumping – bearing in mind that there is no obligation to follow suit. It follows that the safest leads at this time are Nines and then Jacks.

The best time to foreclose a game is when you are strong in trumps and high cards, as the effect is to initiate that period of play in which suit must be followed and tricks won if possible. It is also necessary to decide whether or not to draw immediately before closing. Do you need six tricks for your purpose, or will five suffice? And which of you is more likely to benefit from the draw of another unseen card?

Sixty Six may be a miniature, but it is a jewel of a game.

10 KLABBERJASS

I can think of no better introduction to this game than that of my esteemed card correspondent Robin Goodfellow, who writes: 'Klabberjass, which masquerades under a number of different names, must be, next to Bridge, the most widely known game in the world. It is current in almost every capital where European cards are used. Its spread is undoubtedly due to the emigration of Jewish people into the cities of the western world. Every properly brought up Jewish boy of at least the last generation would know something about *Klobiosh*, even if he did not actively indulge in it. It is also widely played by East Londoners of gentile origin. It has a distinct air of Mittel-Europa about it and I am inclined to believe, with Ely Culbertson, that its birthplace was probably Budapest, although it undoubtedly evolved from the earlier, and simpler, game of Jass.'

Jass – pronounced Yass – is a game much played in Switzerland, though considered to be of Dutch origin. The word means Jack, while klabber means 'clubs' (see also Klaverjass in *Teach Yourself Card Games for Four*). Under the name Kalabriasz it will be familiar to all readers of Damon Runyon, having been probably the most popular game on Broadway before the advent of Gin Rummy. Under the name Belote it will be known to habitués of French bistros and lovers of Byrrh and *boule*. In the Netherlands it is called Smoosjass and in Hungary Alsös. In short, Klabberjass is a centuries-old game of middle European Jewish origin, which has by expansion become one of the most popular pastimes of the western world.

Before starting, it should be noted that the games listed above all differ from one another in many but minor details, and that no two accounts of Klabberjass itself agree in every respect. For this reason I have noted certain rules as options or variants. Beginners should start with the plainest version, and subsequently add optional extras according to taste and previous agreement.

The game

Cards. Standard 32-card pack.

Deal. Whoever cuts the lower card (A K Q J T 9 8 7) deals first, and the deal alternates thereafter until one player reaches a score of 500, which ends the game. Deal six cards each in two batches of three. Place the remainder face down to form a stock. Turn the top card face up and place it beside the stock. The suit of this card is the preferred suit for trumps, but will not necessarily be accepted as such.

Object. After the bidding each player will receive three more cards and play nine tricks. Whoever accepts or nominates the trump suit (the 'maker') thereby undertakes to win the greater number of points for tricks and melds. Trick-points are scored by capturing certain cards with point-values, as shown below. A meld is a sequence of three or more cards in the same suit, or the King and Queen of trumps, known as *bella.*

Rank and value of cards. In non-trump suits cards rank A T K Q J 9 8 7 – note the high position of the Ten. In trumps, the highest card is the Jack, known as Jass, second-highest Nine, known as Menel (accent on the second syllable), then Ace and so on down to the Seven. Cards also have point-values, credited to the player winning them in tricks, as follows:

Jass	20 = Jack of trumps	
Menel	14 = Nine of trumps	
Ace	11 each	*in every suit*
Ten	10 each	
King	4 each	
Queen	3 each	
(Jack)	2 each	*except in trumps*
(Nine)	0	
Eight	0	*in every suit*
Seven	0	

Melds. A sequence of three cards in the same suit counts 20, a sequence of four or more counts 50. The sequential order of cards is A K Q J T 9 8 7 in every suit. (Thus Q–J–T is a sequence of three even though the ranks may not be adjacent in trick-taking power.) The King and Queen of trumps together ('bella') score 20. Melds are not counted until both players have nine cards, and only the player with the best sequence may score for sequences.

Bidding. The rank and value of cards and melds have been described first because bidding can only be carried out on the assessment of one's chances of winning more points than the opponent. It is to be noted that the total value of all the scoring cards in the pack is 152, though not all will be in play, and that the winning of the last trick carries a bonus of 10.

Elder hand starts the bidding by announcing one of three things:

1. *Accept.* In which case he accepts the preferred suit as trumps and becomes the maker.
2. *Schmeiss* (pronounced *shmice*) This is a proposal to abandon the deal. If younger accepts it, the hands are thrown in and there is a new deal. If he refuses, elder is obliged to accept the preferred suit as trump and so become the maker.
3. *Pass.* This is a refusal to become the maker with the preferred suit as trump. Now younger has the same choices: he may accept, schmeiss, or pass. If he passes, elder may either nominate another suit as trump, thereby becoming the maker, or pass. In the latter event, younger may also nominate a suit or pass. If both pass this time, the hands are abandoned and a new deal made.

Play. When one player has become the maker, the dealer deals another batch of three cards to each player from the top of the stock, so that each has nine. Then he takes the bottom card of the stock and places it face up on the top. This card is for information only and has no part in the play. (The purpose of this curious manoeuvre is to ensure that neither player has had the unfair advantage of being the only one to see the bottom card, which may be accidentally or otherwise observed during the deal.)

Dix, pronounced *deece,* is the Seven of trumps if the preferred trump was accepted. If either player has this card he may exchange if for the turned trump-card at any time before the first trick is led. This privilege cannot apply if a different suit was entrumped.

Melds. Before elder leads to the first trick, scores are made for sequences if either player holds any. Only the player who holds the best sequence may score, and he is thereby entitled to score for as many as he shows. (The relevant cards must be revealed.) The best sequence is the one of greatest length; if equal in length, the one with the highest card; if still equal, the one in the trump suit. If neither is in trumps, that of elder hand prevails. Note that the dix may be exchanged either before or after melds are declared, depending on whether the Seven or the card taken is required for a sequence. (Whether or not it is permissible to (a) count the Seven in a sequence of 7–8–9 and then (b) change it for (say) a turned Ace to make and also score another sequence of A–K–Q is a point on which I can find no authority, but I suggest that this should be disallowed.) Bella, if held, is not yet declared.

Tricks. Elder leads to the first trick and the winner of each trick leads to the next. It is obligatory to follow suit, and if a trump is led the second must play a higher trump if he can. A player unable to follow suit is obliged to trump if he can. (In short: you must try to win the trick if the lead is of trumps or a suit in which you are void.)

Bella. If either player holds the King and Queen of trumps he may score 20 by announcing 'bella' upon playing the second of them to a trick.

Last trick. Whoever wins the last trick (sometimes known as *stich,* pronounced *stish*) scores 10 points for it.

Score. Each player announces the total he has made for cards captured in tricks, stich, melds and bella (if any). If the maker has more than his opponent, each counts towards game exactly the amount he has made. If the maker has less, he is said to have 'gone bête' (pronounced and sometimes spelt *bate*); he scores nothing, but his opponent counts towards game the combined total made by both players in that deal. If both have taken the same amount, the maker is 'half bête': he scores nothing, and his opponent scores only the amount he himself has made. The game ends when either player, at the end of a deal, has reached or exceeded a previously agreed total, usually 500.

Variants. Amongst variations and additional rules followed in different countries and localities, the following may be adopted in whole or part.

1. The bid of schmeiss is a comparatively recent addition to the game and may be ignored by purists, though most American and British players like it.
2. In making trumps, first preference is always on clubs and second on the suit of the card turned, if different. This variant is recommended, as it increases demands on good judgement and is in keeping with the name of the game – which, as we have seen, means 'Jack of clubs'.
3. If the suit of first preference has been rejected by both players, either may make a bid of no trump (*sans atout*), which takes precedence over a bid in suit and may be used to overcall it. In this case there is no Jass or Menel, cards rank A T K Q J 9 8 7 in every suit, and each player's final score for the deal is doubled – which makes it attractive to bid no trump on a safe hand, but expensive to go bête on a bad one. If one player bids no trump, the other can overcall him by bidding 'grand' (*tout atout*). In this case there is a Jass and Menel in every suit – in other words, cards rank J 9 A T K Q 8 7 in each suit, and all Jacks are worth 20 and all Nines 14. Otherwise it is played as no trump and also scores double. Grand may only be bid to overcall a previous bid of no trump.
4. In the event of equality for best sequence, the result is a tie and neither may score, instead of declaring elder's to be better by virtue of his position. This is not recommended, as sequences are rare enough already without making them even harder to score.

5. Sometimes a sequence of five or more is valued at 100 points instead of 50 (which is retained for a sequence of four). But such sequences occur so rarely that it hardly seems worth the bother.
6. One source refers to a bonus of 40 for winning all the tricks. It seems reasonable to recognise some sort of bonus for this feat, though the figure quoted would appear to be lifted straight out of Piquet.
7. In the game of Belote (in which there is no bid of schmeiss) additional melds may be scored. Sequences of three count 20, of four 50, and of five or more 100. Also, whoever has the best four of a kind (a *carré* or quartet) may score for any and all quartets he may show, valued thus: four Jacks 200, Nines 150, Aces, Tens, Kings or Queens 100, lower ranks not counting. Game is usually at least 1000 points.
8. If, during the course of play, either player considers that he has reached the target score on melds and/or counting cards so far captured in tricks, he may claim 'out' and end the game immediately – provided that he has already won at least one trick (Belote rule). If he is wrong, he loses the game. Otherwise he wins, even if his opponent has a higher total.

Suggestions for play

Nearly all points are scored for cards won in tricks plus 10 for stich. A whole game may pass without the appearance of a bella or of more than two or three small sequences, and these therefore hardly need to be taken into account in the bidding, unless you are dealt one to start with.

Although the theoretical maximum number of trick-points is 162, it is impossible for all the value-cards to be in play in one deal. In practice, the average number of points in play per deal lies between 100 and 120, of which the maker, if he wins, should expect to score 80–90 against the loser's 20–30. If the game were played with a compulsory trump and no opportunity to pass, each player would expect to take an average of 50–60 points per deal. Since you are called upon to bid on only two thirds of your final hand, you ought to hold 30–40 points in high prospective trumps and supporting Ace-Tens before accepting the preferred suit or nominating another.

It is possible to bid successfully on a hand containing as little as a singleton Jass and two Aces or an Ace–Ten. But this does not mean that all hands are playable. The more expert players become, the more hands they tend to throw in. It does not take more than a few rounds of the game to discover how easily some weak-looking hands win while others, apparently quite promising, fall at the first fence. It is easy enough to recognise a strong hand when you see one, but takes practice to know whether or not to pass or play on something less clear cut. Beginners, I think, should play boldly. You will learn much more from bidding and losing than from passing and never knowing.

In assessing the hand look first for the dix (Seven) of the turned card, unless the latter is an Eight, which is not worth having. In any prospective trump suit it is imperative to hold either the Jack or an accompanied Nine, with preferably an Ace or Ten for company. Do not play a trump suit containing the Ace or Ace–Ten as highest cards, except in the unlikely circumstance of their being accompanied by at least two others of the suit, as there is too great a chance of losing one or more big ones to Jass or Menel in your opponent's hand. Nor be tempted into entrumping a suit just because you have been dealt the King and Queen, worth 20 for bella. If you have a mediocre hand including bella, or a sequence in any suit, the extra value may be just enough to make up either for weaknesses in the hand, or a stout opposition. But never bank on being dealt the marriage partner to a King or Queen already in hand, or a specific card required for a sequence. The odds are more than 7 to 1 against.

A two-card prospective trump including Jass or Menel is sufficient if adequately supported in plain suits, and the mathematical odds favour the appearance of a third in the last part of the deal. (In theory, that is. It never seems to happen to me; but then, I am not one of Dame Fortune's favourites.)

In non-trumps the best holding is an unaccompanied Ace or Ace–Ten, and there is even a goodish chance (4 to 3 in favour) of winning a trick with an ace-less Ten provided that the suit is not held so long as to risk being trumped. A long plain suit, say four or more, is not good for tricks unless it contains low cards which can be used to weaken the opposing trumps – bearing in mind the obligation to trump a suit in which one is void. A void suit in the prospective bidder's hand is a mixed blessing for the same reason. It must, for safety, be accompanied by long trumps, otherwise it will be used to weaken the trump holding.

Younger hand may always bid with greater boldness than elder, since elder's pass is suggestive of weakness. Younger is also in a better position to schmeiss on a hand which is not good for a straightforward acceptance of the turned suit but in which that suit is the only one that stands any chance of succeeding. The fact that elder has passed may justify this move. Elder himself should be very wary of schmeissing, except as a bluff on a good hand, which of course runs the danger of not being called. Otherwise the danger is that younger will accept the schmeiss and prove to hold a fistful of trumps himself.

If you have the lead as maker, your normal strategy on a reasonable hand will be to draw trumps first, partly to test the situation and partly to clear the way for Aces and Tens in plain suits. With a short trump suit or one headed by a tenace (Jack, Ace or Nine, Ten) it is preferable to lead a short plain suit with solid top cards. If you feel that your opponent might hold too many trumps, force them out by leading worthless cards from a long plain suit.

When leading trumps, it is worth starting with the Jack if there is a chance of seizing the Ace or Ten thereby, but (of course) it is dangerous to lead the Nine, Ace or Ten if you lack anything higher. Much of the interest of the game derives from the peculiar positions – third and fourth highest – of the high-scoring Ace and Ten of trumps.

With an average holding of two cards in each suit, it is desirable to win with Aces and Tens as soon as the opportunity arises. If (say) an Eight is led into your Ace/King, it is best to assure yourself of the Ace while you can, rather than hold it back in the hope of catching the Ten with it.

Illustrative deals

First deal. Our two players are Aaron and Bechstein, of whom the latter deals as follows and turns up ♡A:

Aaron ♠K ♡9 7 ♣T J ◇A
Bechstein ♠7 ♡J T 8 ♣Q 8 7

As elder, Aaron has the Menel of the turned suit and can take the Ace by way of the dix. His hand is worth 35 in cards worth counting, and he accepts the turned suit. After three more cards are dealt, and ♠8 turned for information, the hands are:

Aaron ♠A K ♡9 A ♣A T J ◇A 9
Bechstein ♠7 ♡J T 8 ♣K Q 8 7 ◇T

Neither player has improved his trump holding, and it is interesting to note that Bechstein was dealt three trumps including the Jass. With a short trump suit headed only by the second highest, Aaron leads clubs in the hope of retrieving his Ace and Ten before drawing trumps. He takes 21 points on the first two tricks, but then loses his Jack to Bechstein's King (worth a point more than taking it with the Queen). Given the initiative, Bechstein now plans to make the most of his comparatively long trumps. He starts aggressively with the Jass, drawing ♡A for 31 points and the certain knowledge that Aaron has only the Menel in hand, which he next forces out by leading ♡8. Now void of trumps, Aaron plays his Aces, gaining 32 card-points in the process, and continues with ◇9. This Bechstein trumps with his Ten, and concludes with ♣Q, drawing ♠K plus 10 for the last trick. Aaron has just succeeded in his bid, taking 67 to Bechstein's 64. The latter was lucky to hold not only more trumps than his opponent, but also more cards in the same long suit.

Second deal. Aaron turns up ♠T, having dealt:

Bechstein ♠K 9 7 ♡A K ◇T
Aaron ♠J 8 ♡T 9 8 ♣A

Bechstein has three trumps and access to bella by means of the dix. He therefore accepts the turned suit, in which, it will be noted, Aaron holds the top card. The information card, after completion of the hands to the following, is ♢K:

Bechstein ♠9 K Q ♡A K ♣T K ♢T 9
Aaron ♠J 8 ♡T 9 8 ♣A 8 ♢Q 8

After hearing Aaron declare his sequence in hearts for 20, Bechstein leads. He must allow his clubs and diamonds to be led into, as either Ten could fall needlessly to an Ace if led. He therefore decides to force out any high trumps by means of ♠Q, and is fortunate enough to bring the Jass down, leaving his Menel in charge. He can be sure that the Ace and Ten are not in play, otherwise Aaron would have played one of them and held back the Jass for better things, such as catching the Menel or winning the stich. Aaron continues with ♢8, which is taken by the Ten. The bidder now returns ♠K, announcing 'bella' and scoring 20. This draws ♠8, which Bechstein can be certain is the last trump in his adversary's hand. The remaining tricks are played like bat and ball. Bechstein wins his game, scoring 49 in tricks plus 10 for stich and 20 for bella, 79 in all, to Aaron's 53 in tricks plus 20 for the sequence, 73 in all. The round totals after two deals are A 140, B 143. And it's anybody's game.

II ECARTE

A fast and exciting game of deceptive simplicity, Ecarté is the comparatively modern form of a centuries-old game called Triomphe or French Ruff. The basic idea is simple. Five cards are dealt to each player, and the object is to win at least three of the tricks played, or preferably all five. What makes it interesting, not to say subtle, is the fact that the hands are not necessarily played with the cards first dealt. Instead, both may draw fresh cards in exchange for worthless rejects until one player is satisfied with his hand, at which point play begins. All the fun, and much of the skill, lies in deciding when to stop exchanging and start playing.

Although Ecarté is for two, and makes a pleasant home game for couples who have no need to pay each other[6], it has spent most of its long life as a rather vigorous casino gambling game. One player is put up by the house to take on any and all comers one at a time, while onlookers are able to lay bets on the outcome. Ecarté supplanted Triomphe as the premier game of Parisian casinos early in the 19th century, and even up to 1970 could still be found in a few French establishments, which is not bad going for an industry whose native products are more prone than most to the importation of American substitutes.

It also became popular in English clubs during the last century, and the rules which follow are essentially those of the English form of the game as promulgated by the Portland Club and expounded by 'Cavendish' in the most authoritative monograph to have appeared on the subject.[7]

---

6. Strip Ecarté is a much more workable game than Strip Poker. Ecarté actually means 'discarded', but the reference is to the business of exchanging cards before play.
7. Cavendish, *Ecarté* – 6th Edition (LONDON, 1878).

The game

Cards. Use a 32-card pack, with nothing lower than Seven. It is convenient to use two packs, one being shuffled while the other is dealt, and to have five counters each as a scoring aid (though this is not essential).

Deal. Decide first dealer by any agreed means, after which the deal alternates. Shuffle, offer for cutting, then deal five cards each in batches of two and three. This may be 2+3 or 3+2 on your first deal, but whichever it is you must stick to for the rest of your deals in the same game. Place the undealt cards face down to one side to form a stock. Face the top card and lay it on the table beside the stock. The suit of the turn-up is the trump suit for the deal. If the turn-up is a King, the dealer marks 1 point for it.

Object. In each deal the object is to win three or four tricks (the *point*), for 1 point, or all five (the *vole*), for 2. The game is won by the first to reach 5 points after several deals. If counters are used, each places five on the table at his own left and transfers one to his right for each point marked.

Rank. Cards rank from high to low in each suit as follows: K Q J A T 9 8 7. Note the intermediate position of the Ace.

Discarding. If elder hand is satisfied with his cards, he may begin play by leading to the first trick. If not, he may *propose* a change of cards by calling 'Cards'. In this event, younger may either accept the proposal, in which case both can exchange cards as explained below, or else refuse, in which case elder must lead. (It should be noted that if elder plays without proposing, and loses, he loses double; similarly, younger loses double if he refuses the first proposal and fails to win.)

If the proposal is accepted, elder rejects face down from his hand as many cards as he does not want, announcing this number clearly. Younger does likewise, and then deals from the top of the stock first as many cards as elder needs to complete his hand, then as many as he needs himself. Now the same situation obtains. Elder may play or propose; if he proposes, younger may accept or refuse; if he accepts, more cards are exchanged in the same manner. It should be noted that younger, having accepted a proposal, thereby obliges elder to discard at least one, but need not himself exchange any if he then decides not to.

This continues until either play begins or cards run out, in which case play must begin anyway. Note that the turn-up is not part of the stock and may not be dealt as a replacement. If not enough cards remain to fill both players' hands, such cards as do remain go to elder. If either player is forced to retrieve one or more of his last discards because not enough replacements remain in stock, he must do so before seeing the cards he is dealt.

Marking the King. If either player holds the King of trumps he may mark one point for it provided that he announces 'King' before playing a card to the first trick, or as he does so if he plays it to that trick. If he fails to announce it in time he is too late, as the King may not be marked in retrospect. If marking the King brings a player's score to 5, the hand is not played out.

Play. Elder leads to the first trick, and the winner of each trick leads to the next. The second player must not only follow suit if able, but also win the trick if he can. If unable to follow suit, he must play a trump if he has any. The trick is won with the higher card of the suit led, or the higher trump if any are played. (In leading to the first trick, it is traditional for elder to announce the suit of the card he leads.)

Score. The winner marks 1 point for taking three or four tricks, 2 points for taking all five. But if elder played without proposing and lost, younger scores 2 whether he took three, four or five tricks. Similarly, elder scores 2 if younger lost after refusing elder's first proposal. Note that this increased value applies only if the hand was played with the cards originally dealt, no discards having been made, and only if the player who accepted his hand as good fails to take three tricks.

Revoke. If a player revokes, by failing to follow suit or win the trick or play a trump when able and required to do so, his opponent may upon discovery of the offence call for the hand to be replayed with the same cards. If the offender wins, he scores in the usual way but first subtracts one point from his total as a penalty. If he loses, there is no penalty.

Game. The game may be lengthened by agreeing that a rubber is won by the first player to win two games, for which there is a bonus of two points. Alternatively, play up to a previously agreed total of game points such as 5 or 10. For this purpose it may be preferred to count 1 game point if the opponent has scored 3 or 4, 2 if he scored 1 or 2, and 3 if he scored nothing at all.

Notes on play

The whole point of the game lies in deciding, when you have the choice, whether to play with the cards held or to propose (or accept a proposal) to change cards. Roughly speaking, a hand is playable when it contains at least three cards which are trumps or Kings. Looked at another way, it is advisable to discard all cards which are neither trumps nor Kings, and not to discard fewer than three. But there are exceptions to this principle, governed by such factors as whether you are younger or elder, whether or not you hold the King of trumps, and the state of the score.

From a score of love-all, there are certain types of hand upon which elder's best move is to play rather than propose. Such hands are called *jeux de règle*, 'obligatory plays', for the reason that, in casino play, the house player is obliged to play if dealt one of them – otherwise he is likely to find himself rapidly redundant and without a reference. It should go without saying that anything better than the following minimum *jeux de règles* is equally 'obligatory'. On the other hand, completely mechanical play is boring in its predictability, and more excitement may be squeezed out of playing the occasional shaky hand or sometimes proposing on a good one.

Three or more trumps. No matter how low they are, or what the non-trumps may be, a hand with three trumps is worth playing. Remember that there are only eight cards in each suit, and that one trump – the turn-up – is out of play, thus making it unlikely that younger will have more than one of the other four trumps. Best procedure is to lead the highest trump. If it is not taken you will almost certainly win three trump tricks, and if it is you will expect to win the other two trumps and make an eventual third trick by leading a suit your opponent cannot follow.

Two-trump hands. A hand with two trumps is playable if the other three cards are all of the same suit, or include a King or a guarded Queen. From the first of these, lead the highest card of the plain suit, and keep doing so at every opportunity. Two trumps and a singleton King is playable provided that the other two cards, if of different suits, are not both lower than Ten. Lead the King, unless the other two are of the same suit, in which case lead the higher of them. From two trumps and a guarded Queen (*ie* a Queen accompanied by at least one other of her suit), lead the Queen. Other two-trump hands are playable if the three non-trumps are generally high and not all of different suits, even down to Jack of one suit and Ten, Nine of another. Generally, lead the higher of the two-card plain suit.

One-trump hands. Playable if they contain K–Q–J of another suit, or if the other four cards are of the same suit and include the King, which should be led. Also playable is a hand consisting of a trump, a Queen, and another Queen twice guarded, from which the guarded Queen should be led. Risky is one trump plus two guarded Queens. At least one of the guards should be not lower than Ten.

No-trump hands. A hand devoid of trumps is playable if it contains three Queens or at least four court cards, provided that they are not all Jacks. (But four Jacks and another trump is playable – see two-trump hands.)

By and large, younger may refuse a proposal if he holds a hand that would be a *jeu de règle* with the positions reversed, though some patterns need to be somewhat stronger. Although the fact that elder proposes suggests that his hand is too weak to play, this does not make younger's that much stronger by comparison, since he is likely to be forced into trumping earlier and lacks the initiative to start with his strongest plain suit. In particular, a one-trump hand containing K–Q–J of another suit only merits a refusal if the fifth card is also a court, while a two-trumper with three in a plain suit similarly requires the best plain card to be a court.

Possession of the King of trumps is a key factor in play, as it scores as much as winning the point in its own right, which may prove enough for game, and also increases one's chance of winning the vole whilst ensuring defence against it. The latter considerations also apply to the Queen of trumps when the King has been turned up. It follows that a hand qualifying as a *jeu de règle*, or a refusal, may nevertheless justify one or two discards for the sake of the vole. For example, suppose spades are trumps and you hold

♠K Q ♡K Q ♣7

Although you have a certain four tricks and possible vole as it stands, you may propose in the hope of discarding the Seven and drawing a spade, heart or high card in its place. If refused, you will score 2 for the point in any case.

The *jeux de règle* should be known by heart, as an astute player may learn much from your indecisiveness or air of calculation if you do not play, propose, accept or refuse immediately and evenly. For much the same reason, the astute player, having dealt, will not look at his own cards until elder has made his first decision, in order to avoid giving anything away by inadvertent grimaces (or whoops of delight). And it is the height of folly to give way to force of habit by arranging one's cards in rank and suit.

Normal procedure in play is to lead the top card from one's longest plain suit. This is the suit most likely to force younger into trumping, and it is a general principle that where both players hold the same number of trumps the one first forced is most weakened. If the lead holds, continue the suit until it is trumped; but if you also hold the top trump it may profitably be led second before the forcing suit is continued. Trumps should be led only if four or more are held, or with three in hand if the top two are consecutive. From two trumps, a singleton King and two low cards, lead one of the low cards if both are of the same suit, and the King if both are different. With weak trumps and high plain cards, it is well to lead the high cards and keep changing the suit to avoid being trumped. If you manage to win the first three tricks in this way, lead the trump fourth with a view to the vole.

So far we have considered hands strong enough to have been led from without proposing. What happens when you have to lead from a poor hand on which you have proposed, but have been refused, depends on whether the hand is only poor, or so desperate that the vole may be won against you. In the latter case the important thing is to take a trick as soon as possible. Lead any King, or, if you have none, your highest single card – 'single' in the sense of being the only one in its suit. It is not advisable to lead from a guarded plain suit, such as Q–A, as you have more chance of making a trick from it if your opponent leads into that suit. If the situation is not desperate, prefer to lead one of two consecutive cards in a suit rather than from a non-sequential holding of high cards.

If you win the first two tricks and find your opponent out of trumps, always continue with a non-trump King if you have one, and then lead a trump fourth. He will then prefer to discard from your King-suit if possible in order to preserve a possible defence in some other suit against the fifth lead. If then your fifth card is of the same suit as your King, you will win the vole. If not, you may gain nothing extra in the short run, but will have played consistently and so stand a better chance of succeeding with the ruse when the opportunity next presents itself. Otherwise, an astute opponent will notice that you only play King-then-trump when the King is guarded, and will not fall for discarding the wrong suit to the trump lead.

If left with a trump and a plain card when three tricks have been divided, lead the plain card if you have won two tricks, the trump if only one. This gives you the best opportunity of winning the point.

The best time to mark the King is when about to play to the first trick. This gives younger the advantage of withholding useful information that might otherwise have influenced elder's lead. There is rarely much point in sinking the King (deliberately refraining from marking it). Younger may do so when he stands at three towards game against elder's four and elder plays without proposing, as younger will score two and the game anyway if elder loses, and will lose anyway if elder wins the point. Similarly, elder may sink when he has three to younger's four and younger refuses the first proposal. If when your opponent stands at four points you lack the King and it is not turned up, you should be prepared to play on a riskier hand than normally, as the more exchanging you allow to take place, the greater his chance of winning outright by drawing the King. In these circumstances it doesn't matter if you play immediately or refuse the first proposal, as a score of two is no better than of one to the player with four. Finally, if your opponent proposes when he stands at four points to your three, refuse if you have even an outside chance of winning the point. It is true that he will win the game if you fail, but to have proposed at all at such a score indicates a very weak hand.

Unless, of course, he was bluffing. And this is the point at which all clever stratagems come to nought, for Ecarté, more than any other trick-taking game except Le Truc, is wide open to the sort of intuitive and bluffing play which tends to unnerve 'calculating' players by tying them up in knots.

Illustrative game

First deal. Bertrand deals, the first card going to Armand. He turns up ♢A, and the hands are:

A: ♢J 9 ♠K ♣T 8 *proposes*
B: ♢Q ♠T ♡Q T 7 *accepts*

The new hands are:

A: ♢J 9 ♠K ♡J ♣7 *proposes*
B: ♢Q ♠J A 8 ♣J *accepts*

And again:

A: ♢J 9 ♠K ♣K 9 *plays*
B: ♢Q 8 7 ♡K ♠9

The play proceeds: ♣K ♢*7*, ♡K ♢*9*, ♣9 ♢*8*, ♠9 ♠*K*, at which point they have two tricks each. Bertrand's Queen wins the last trick and gives him the point. Had Armand played his original hand he would have won, but by constant exchanging he permitted Bertrand to gain three trumps to his own two. Score: A = 0, B = 1.

Second deal. Armand deals, turning up ♡K for which he marks a point.

B: ♡T ♣Q T ♢9 ♠9 *proposes*
A: ♡J ♣J ♢K Q ♠8 *refuses*

Armand considers Bertrand's proposal to be made from weakness and a desire not to lose the initiative, and refuses on the strength of his four court cards. But Bertrand, despite his feeble hand, correctly refrains from leading his guarded suit and succeeds in winning the first, third and fourth tricks as follows: ♠*9* ♠8, ♢9 ♢*K*, ♢Q ♡*T*, ♣*Q* ♣J, ♣T ♡*J*. Bertrand marks two for having won after a refusal, and the scores are now A = 1, B = 3.

Third deal. Bertrand, before turning up ♢9, deals:

A: ♢J T ♠J ♡Q ♣A *proposes*
B: ♢Q ♠K 9 ♡8 7 *accepts*

Then after exchanging:

A: ♢J T 7 ♣7 ♡9 *proposes*
B: ♢K Q ♠K A T *refuses*

Bertrand, if he had the lead, would hope Armand had not more than two trumps and would play for the vole. As it is, he thinks he has good prospects after a second request for cards. But not so. Armand leads ♢J and Bertrand announces the King as he plays it. There follows ♠K ♢7, ♡9 ♢*Q*, ♠A ♢7, ♣7 ♠T, and Armand gains the point. Score now: Armand = 2, Bertrand = 4.

Fourth deal. Armand deals, turning up ♠T:

B: ♢K Q ♡Q T ♣7 *proposes*
A: ♠K ♣K Q ♡J 8 *refuses*

If Bertrand proposes needing only one point to game, Armand's hand gives him more than a fighting chance. Upon trumping the first trick, Armand marks his King: ♢K ♠*K*, ♣*K* ♣7, ♣Q and Armand wins the point. In leading the Queen rather than switching to hearts, Armand hopes that Bertrand either had been dealt no trumps, or, if he were, could still follow suit to clubs, in view of the fact that it was the lowest of all he had thrown to the King. Score: Armand = 4, Bertrand = 4.

Fifth deal. Bertrand deals, turning up ♣8:

A: ♣7 ♡K Q ♠Q 9 *plays*
B: ♣T ♡Q T ♢K Q

Armand now plays to the score, preventing Bertrand from drawing the King (if he had it, he would already have announced it and won), and hoping his opponent has not more than one trump if any. It pays off. The play proceeds: ♡*K* ♡9, ♠Q ♣*T*, ♢K ♣7, ♡*Q* ♡J – giving Armand the point and the game.

12

LE TRUC

Le Truc has been characterised as 'little French Poker' and is supposed to be a gambling game; but this makes it sound dreadfully earnest and I think it is much better played for fun, especially when you are feeling in need of light relief. Hilarity is not a quality normally associated with the playing of cards, but if you do happen to be looking for a game that can properly be described as sidesplitting, this is it.

As here reported, Le Truc is a game for two or four that used to be very popular in Provence. The present account is borrowed from Sid Sackson's interpretation (in his *Gamut of Games*[8]) of a slightly less than lucid description taken from a French book published in 1912. The four-hand version has much in common with the Latin American game of El Truco and with a curious Breton game – played with a special pack of basically Spanish cards – called L'Aluette or La Luette. In these, partners are allowed to convey to each other an indication of the cards they hold by means of an elaborate system of winks, nods and sundry grimaces, which add even more to the fun. It is also related to the old English game of Put or Putt, which I might have preferred to describe for chauvinistic reasons, but it is frankly less varied and more staid.

If it means anything at all, *le truc* is equivalent to 'the knack'. Let this be taken as a warning that this is in no sense a game of card skill. It is entirely a game of bluff, counter-bluff, and counter-counter-bluff.

The game

Cards. Use a standard 32-card pack, lacking all cards numbered lower than Seven.

8. Sackson, *A Gamut of Games* (Nelson, LONDON, 1974).

Deal. Take turns to deal, and shuffle thoroughly between deals. Deal three cards each, one at a time.

Rank. Cards rank 7 8 A K Q J T 9. The Sevens are highest, followed by the Eights, and the Nines are lowest of all. Suits are entirely irrelevant. The higher of two cards wins, and if both are equal the trick is tied.

Game. Theoretically, the object in each deal is to win two of the three tricks – or, if any tricks are tied, to be the first to win a trick at all. In practice, it is to bluff your opponent into thinking that you can win, by raising the value of the game so high that he concedes defeat before all the tricks are played. In this event you win whether you have good cards or not, and need not show what they were. A game is won by the first player to reach 12 points, which can be done in one deal but may take several.

Calling. Elder hand leads to the first trick, but if he is (or pretends to be) not satisfied with his hand he may first propose a fresh deal by calling 'Cards'. If younger agrees, both must reject their entire hands face down and are then dealt three more one at a time from the top of the pack. Only one such redeal may be made.

Tricks. The rules of trick play are that the second player need not follow suit but may play any card he likes, and the trick is won by the higher ranking of the two cards played. If they are of the same rank, the trick is tied and put to one side. The winner of a trick leads to the next, but in the event of a tie the same leader leads again. If the first trick is tied, the deal is won by the first player to win a subsequent trick; if the first is won and the second tied, the winner of the first wins the deal.

Play. Elder hand leads by playing any card and announcing 'One'. This refers to the value of the game, representing the amount to be scored by the winner if the game is not subsequently increased. Younger now has a choice of play. He may throw his hand in, leaving elder to score 1 point. Or he may reply to the trick, leaving the value still at 1 point but staying in the game. Or he may offer to double by saying 'Two if I play'.

In this event, elder may accept, in which case younger plays his card and the game is now worth 2 points to the eventual winner, or he may refuse, in which case younger wins 1 point without further play and the deal is at an end. Thereafter, each person on his turn to play a card, whether leading or following to a trick, has exactly the same options: he may throw his hand in, leaving the other to score the current game value; he may play, leaving the value unaltered; or he may offer to double by saying 'Four if I play' (or 'Eight' as the case may be). In reply to an offer to double, the opponent may either accept by saying 'Play', in which case the value is doubled, or concede defeat immediately, in which case the other wins just the amount he was seeking to double. There is, however, a restriction on doubling, as follows:

'*My remainder*'. Neither player is permitted to double if a win would yield him more than 12 points, e.g. from 8 to 16, or from 4 to 8 if he already has 4 or more towards game. Instead, a player wishing to double beyond the limit may bid 'My remainder', which merely means 'I'm raising the value of the game to as many as I need to make 12, so that I'll win the game if I win this deal'. In this event, his opponent may throw in, as before, and the proposed increase does not take effect. Alternatively, he may (and invariably will, if he does not concede), counter by bidding '*My* remainder', no matter how many points he needs to reach 12. After that, it follows that the winner of the deal wins the game outright.

Illustrative deals

To clarify the mechanism of play, here are some illustrative deals between Alain and Bernard. Bernard deals as follows:

To A: K K Q
To B: J 9 9

Alain proposes cards; Bernard accepts, and deals:

To A: 7 T T
To B: 8 A J

A leads T, announces 'One'
B; 'Two if I play?' (A accepts). Play J and takes.
B; 'Four if I play?' (A accepts). Leads 8.
A; 'Eight if I play?' (B refuses)

Result: Alain wins 4 points. It will be noticed that if Bernard had not been frightened out he would have won against the cards actually held.

Now Alain deals as follows:

To B: 8 8 9
To A: 7 8 K

B; leads 8, announces 'One'.
A; 'Two if I play?' (B accepts). A ties with 8.
B; 'Four if I play?', (A accepts). B plays 8.
A; 'My remainder?' (B refuses).

Alain scores 4, bringing his total to 10 against Bernards' zero. Had Bernard accepted, Alain would have taken with his Seven, winning the deal (and the game) anyway.

Now Bernard deals:

To A: 7 K 9
To B: A J T

Alain proposes an exchange of cards, which Bernard refuses, his bluff being somewhat greater than his opponent's.

A leads 7, announces 'One'.
B plays T, losing the trick.
A; 'My remainder?'
B; '*My* remainder'.
A plays K; B takes with Ace.
B plays T and wins the trick and the game, to Alain's 11 points.

Notes on play

As will be seen from the above examples, very little in Le Truc depends upon the cards held – nearly all depends upon the way they are played, and the extent to which players are prepared to bluff each other and take chances. For this reason there is little that can be given by way of strategic advice. The one important thing to remember is the desirability of winning the first trick, because that will win the deal if either of the other two tricks is tied. (In French, a tied trick is described as *pourri*, meaning 'rotten' – or, literally, 'putrefied'.) The power of the bluff cannot be overestimated, a point not to be forgotten when your opponent has just led a card which, from your own holding, you know will win him the deal. Do not automatically throw your cards in. *He* cannot see your hand, and you may yet frighten him out by offering to double.

PART III
GAMES OF EQUAL OPPORTUNITY

In traditional card games, each player is dealt a hand of cards at random and does not know what his opponent holds. Although one may hold better cards than the other, neither can know this in advance, and, in the best games, the player with the worse cards may yet win through the application of greater skill. This accounts for the fundamental difference between card games and board games such as Chess and Draughts; in the latter both start with equal positions and each always knows what the other is doing. But some card games have been devised in which both players start with exactly the same cards, or exactly complementary cards, or with no cards at all but exactly equal access to them. In these games, neither player has any advantage over the other except by way of his personal abilities of calculation, memory, bluff, or whatever. It may come as a surprise to discover how varied such games can be. Poker Squares is based on probabilities, Quintet and Gops on personalities, Challenge, Mate and Abstrac on forward visualisation.

13 POKER SQUARES

This game can be played by any number from one upwards, but it is ideal for two. Poker Squares is the playing-card equivalent of a word game well known under various titles, of which the aptest is 'Wordsworth'. In the word game, each draws a grid of $5 \times 5 = 25$ squares; turns are taken to call out a letter of the alphabet 25 times in all, and everyone enters the letters into their own grid one by one as they are announced – the winner is the player who by the end of the game has succeeded in so arranging them as to form the most and longest words.

In Poker Squares, it is playing cards which are called out one by one, and the winner is the player who, by entering each in the 'best' position as it is called out, succeeds in forming a square whose ten rows and columns produce the highest scoring Poker hands. For those who do not know Poker, hands are described below and illustrated on page 131. The game itself, it may be added, has nothing to do with Poker proper, and is not a bluffing or necessarily a gambling game. In America, at least, Poker Squares was a fad game of (I believe) the early 'twenties, which was eventually displaced in what might be called 'parlour popularity' by the then new craze for crosswords.

Poker hands

A Poker hand is any five cards, by definition. The cards may or may not be related to one another by rank or suit. The more related cards there are, the better the hand. In Poker, the best possible hand is a straight flush, and other hands rank below it in descending order as follows.

Straight flush. Five cards of the same suit and in numerical sequence. Ace may count high or low, so the highest possible is A–K–Q–J–T (sometimes called a royal flush), the lowest 5–4–3–2–A.

Four of a kind (fours). Four cards of the same rank, such as J–J–J–J. The fifth card may be anything.

Full house. Three cards of one rank, and two of another, such as 7–7–7–J–J.

Flush. Any five cards of the same suit not all in numerical sequence; for example ♠A–K–Q–J–9 or ♡Q–8–6–3–2.

Straight. Five cards in numerical sequence but not all of the same suit, with Ace counting high or low ad lib.

Three of a kind (threes). Three cards of the same rank, the other two unmatched.

Two pair. Two cards of the same rank; two of another rank; the fifth unmatched.

One pair. Two of the same rank; the other three unmatched.

Nothing. Five unrelated cards of different suits and ranks.

The game

Cards. Two complete 52-card packs, to be kept separate from each other. It is convenient to use Patience cards because of their smaller size.

Preparation. Each player must have enough table space to enable him to lay out 25 cards in a 5×5 square, and neither player should be able to see his opponent's square. They should therefore sit at different tables, or erect a screen between them. Each player takes a full pack. One player shuffles his thoroughly; the other arranges his in rank and suit order, in such a way as to be able to pick out any named card immediately.

Play. The player with the shuffled pack is the caller. With his pack face down, he turns up the top card and announces what it is. He places this anywhere before him to start his 25-card square, and his opponent takes the same card from his own pack and does likewise in his own space. When both are ready, the caller turns the second card and announces it. This continues until 25 cards have been called, by which time each player will have built up a square consisting of five rows and five columns, each containing five cards. Throughout play, a card that has once been placed in position may not be moved in relation to any other of the square.

Score. When each square is complete both are revealed and scored. Each row and each column earns a score based on either of the following schedules, depending upon which has been agreed beforehand:

HAND	ENGLISH	AMERICAN
Straight flush	30	75 (100 for A–K–Q–J–T)
Four of a kind	16	50
Full house	10	25
Flush	5	20
Straight	12	15
Three of a kind	6	10
Two pair	3	5
One pair	1	2

The English scoring system is based on the relative difficulty of making the various hands in the game of Poker Squares. It is obvious, for example, that no combination of 25 cards can fail to yield at least two flushes, and may yield up to five, whereas if no Fives or Tens appear it will be impossible to form any straights. The flush is therefore more frequently made than the straight, and properly scores less. The American system is based on the relative difficulty of getting the various hands in the game of Poker, which of course is quite irrelevant to the way Poker Squares is played.

Suggestions for play

Although you can start the game fairly methodically, there soon comes a point at which you have to make a choice between alternative possibilities that interfere with each other.

It is convenient to regard your first card as the centre of the square. Let us suppose it is ♣8. If the second card is another Eight, you will naturally lay it side by side to make a pair. If it is another club within the same range for a straight – anything from ♣4 to ♣Q – do likewise, with a view to a straight flush if possible, or a straight *or* a flush if it gets broken up. As a matter of habit, I always build combinations of rank – pairs, threes, full houses and fours – in horizontal rows, and those of suit and sequence in vertical columns. Of course, it doesn't matter which way round you do it. The important thing is to realise that at some stage in the proceedings it may become apparent that the cards turning up fall more naturally into combinations of rank than of suit/sequence. When this happens, it may be advisable to forget the latter and make rank combinations in both directions.

Let's go back to our second card. If it is, say, ♣6, then place it above or below ♣8 and hope that it will develop into a straight or flush or both. If it bears no relation to ♣8 – for example, ♢K – the most methodical place for it is point-to-point, or diagonally adjacent to the Eight. Problems arise if the second card is of the same suit as the first, but not in the same range, such as ♣2 in this case. Should it be aligned with the Eight with a view to a mere flush, or set diagonally against it? A useful point to bear in mind here is that you have five columns (assuming you are using columns of suit-sequences) but only four suits. This gives you one opportunity to attempt to duplicate a flush, or to convert one column into a rubbish row for the disposal of unmatchable cards as they arise during the game. It is useful to keep back a rubbish row for the same purpose too. In this case, you can put the ♣2 into diagonal line with ♣8, and regard both cards as the start of two potential club flushes.

(There is an optional rule, insisted on by some players, to the effect that the second and each subsequent card must be placed edge to edge with a card already in the array. This is unnecessarily restrictive and decreases the skill factor of the game. A similar rule requiring each new card to be placed next to an existing one, but either edge to edge or point to point as preferred, is considerably less restrictive. Circumstances in which it might prove a hardship rarely occur and are difficult even to concoct.)

Suppose, now, our first cards were placed diagonally thus:

◇K
♣8

We now have the beginnings of a discipline for subsequent cards. If the next is ♣J we will place it in the ♣8 column but not in line with ◇K, giving us two clubs in a possible straight, and permitting ◇J, if it occurs, to be matched with both ♣J in the row and ◇K, in the column, for another potential straight flush. A heart or spade would go in a third column, in line with the Eight or King if of the same rank but not otherwise. A completely different card, such as ♠2, therefore extends the King–Eight diagonal. And so on.

Won't both players finish up with the same arrangement if they follow the same methodics? Not necessarily, because they will differ in their treatment of problematical cards, and one may go all out for a straight flush while the other will deem it better odds to break one up for the sake of, say, fours in the other direction. To demonstrate differences of approach, here are two different Poker Squares built up from the same cards, which were called in the following order: ◇9, ♣T, ◇K, ♠3, ♣8, ♠4, ♡2, ♣Q, ♠J, ♡4, ♣J (this card threw a spanner in both players' works!), ♣T, ♡3, ♡8, ◇5, ♡7, ♠9, ♠A, ♡5, ◇3, ♣9, ♣7, ♡9, ♠8, ◇4.

As you will see from Figure 5 (page 134), both played 'methodically' but took different risks as to what might be subsequently turned up, resulting in quite a wide margin of victory for the winner.

♠3	♠8	◇5	♣9	♡2	= 0
♠4	♠T	◇3	♣T	♡4	= 3
♠A	♠9	◇9	♣J	♡8	= 1
♣7	◇4	◇K	♣Q	♡7	= 1
♡9	♠J	♡5	♣8	♡3	= 0
0+	0+	1+	30+	5+	5 = 41 total

♡8	♠J	◇5	♣8	♠A	= 1
♡3	♠T	◇3	♣T	♠3	= 10
♡7	♠9	◇9	♣J	♡9	= 6
♡2	♣7	◇K	♣9	♡5	= 0
♡4	♠8	◇4	♣Q	♠4	= 6
5+	12+	5+	30+	0+	23 = 75 total

FIGURE 5

Two completed Poker Squares

14 QUINTET

The rags-to-riches story of the man who invented *Monopoly* is an integral part of twentieth century mythology, but nobody, to my knowledge, has ever made a fortune out of inventing a card game. And I speak with all the authority of one who has invented several cards games and failed to make a fortune several times over. It is a curious fact that games which really catch on and become established classics, such as Canasta, can never be traced back to one person, whereas personal strokes of creative brilliance, such as Hoffman's Quinto or R. B. Willis's Calypso (both in *Card Games for Four*), are forgotten in the space of a few years. I feel it not without significance that the millionaire who developed modern Contract Bridge, Harold S. Vanderbilt, is now hardly remembered by name, whereas Ely Culbertson, who waged a brilliantly successful publicity campaign to establish it as a world-wide classic, is now as well known as Hoyle.

No doubt I am cracking a nut with a sledgehammer, for I cannot pretend that Quintet is the greatest two-hander ever devised. But it was invented by Hubert Phillips, who was also responsible for the unjustly neglected Contract Whist described in *Card Games for Four*, and in my book that makes it worthy of closer attention. It is a small-scale game of bluff based on Poker hands, and has several points of interest that make it capable of developing into something bigger than the inventor may have envisaged.

The game

Cards. Two separate 32-card packs are used, each consisting of A K Q J T 9 8 7 in each suit.

Deal. Each player takes a complete pack. One shuffles his thoroughly and deals off the top seven cards, face up, leaving himself with 25. The other then removes exactly the same seven cards from his own pack, thereby reducing it in the same way.

Play. Each player now arranges his 25 cards in five Poker hands of five cards each, taking care not to let his opponent see how he is arranging them, and places the five hands in an order of presentation. When both are ready, each player reveals his first hand, and the one showing the better combination scores 3 points. Then the second hands are revealed, and this time the winner scores 4 points. For the third, fourth and fifth hands the winner scores respectively 5, 6 and 7 points. Thus there are 25 points to be played for in all, and it is possible to win by showing the better hand on the last two turns, scoring 6+7 = 13. In the event of a tie on any hand, the appropriate points for that turn are shared equally.

Poker hands

Poker hands are defined and illustrated in the previous chapter on Poker Squares, p 131, but in Quintet additional information is needed about how hands of the same type rank against each other.

Straight flush. As between two straight flushes, the one with the higher top card wins. Thus A–K–Q–J–T is highest and J–T–9–8–7 lowest. Ties are possible.

Fours. Four of a higher beats four of a lower rank, with Aces best, Sevens lowest.

Full House. The higher-ranking triplet wins. Thus 8–8–8–9–9 beats 7–7–7–A–A.

Flush. Won by the flush with the highest top card, or second highest if equal, and so on. Thus ♠A–J–9–8–7 beats ♡A–T–9–8–7. Ties are possible.

Straight. Won by the straight with the higher top card, as are straight flushes. Ties are possible.

Threes. Won by the higher-ranking triplet. Thus 8–8–8–9–T beats 7–7–7–K–A.

Two pair. Won by the hand containing the higher-ranking pair (e.g. J–J–7–7–8 beats 9–9–8–8–A), or second pair if equal, or odd card if still equal (e.g. K–K–Q–Q–8 beats K–K–Q–Q–7). Ties are possible.

One pair. Won by the higher-ranking pair, or, if equal, decided by the highest odd card. Thus Q–Q–A–9–7 beats Q–Q–A–8–7. Ties are possible.

Nothing. Won by the highest-ranking untied card; e.g. A–J–9–8–7 beats A–J–T–9–8. Ties are possible.

Note about straights. When proper Poker is played with a 32-card pack, it is usual to permit the Ace to count either high or low for the purpose of making a straight or straight flush, so that the lowest possible straight is T–9–8–7–A. Phillips does not state whether this applies to Quintet, and the point should be agreed beforehand. It strikes me as an illogical and unnecessary complication; Ace-low straights are therefore ignored in the rest of this chapter.

Illustrative deal

Here is Phillips's own illustration of play. We will call the players Novice and Oldhand. The cards rejected are ♠K, ♡Q–T–8, ♣Q, ◇J–T, leaving as playing hands:

♠A . Q J T 9 8 7
♡A K . J . 9 . 7
♣A K . J T 9 8 7
◇A K Q . . 9 8 7

First hand. Knowing that the game can be won on the last two hands, Novice starts by putting aside the Queen-high straight flush in spades for his fifth hand and his Jack-high clubs for his fourth, reckoning to do no worse than divide the points. Leaving his rubbish for the first hand, he starts by showing a pair: ♠7 ♡7 ♡K ♡J ♡9. Oldhand beats this with a full house: ♠7 ♡7 ◇7 ♡9 ◇9. Score 3–0 in favour of Oldhand.

Second hand. Novice comes up with a flush: ♢K Q 9 8 7. Oldhand counters with four Aces and the ♡J for ballast. Score now 7–0.

Third hand. Novice's four Aces appear next, along with ♣K, and are overtaken by Oldhand's straight flush in clubs, Jack high. Score 12–0. To avoid loss, Novice must now win the last two hands, or at least tie.

Fourth hand. Novice's club straight flush now falls to Oldhand's straight flush in spades, the Queen beating the Jack. Score 18–0.

Fifth hand. Novice brings his sledgehammer Queen-high spade straight flush down upon Oldhand's three King nut, and succeeds in losing by 18 to 7.

Both players, it will be observed, made three hands the same: the Queen and Jack-high straight flushes and the four Aces. The rest were formed into a pair and a flush by Novice, and a full house and three Kings by Oldhand. Correctly anticipating that Novice would leave his best hands for rounds three, four and five, Oldhand put the same hands to use in rounds two, three and four, thus going one better each time and assuring himself of scoring $4+5+6 = 15$ of the 25 points. In theory, of course, Novice might have foreseen Oldhand's line of reasoning and countered it by planning those same hands for rounds one, two and three, netting 12 points straight off and beating the final three Kings with his flush, for a game score of 19 to 6.

Further thoughts

I described Quintet as a game of bluff, which at this stage is not strictly true: a more accurate description would be that it is a game of judgement. To my mind, the need to decide in advance upon the order in which to present the hands makes the game rather restrictive, as all the strategy must be applied before the hands are played. There are several ways in which an element of bluff might be introduced to give the game a little more variety. For instance:

Any order. In this version, the players do not have to predetermine the order of showing hands, except the first. Once the first has been decided, each may select which of the four remaining to show second, and so on of those remaining for the third and subsequent rounds. Taking the illustrative deal already described, for instance, it is possible that Novice might have played a straight flush on the second round, in order to compensate for losing his pair to a full house on the first. Oldhand, foreseeing this manoeuvre, might allow Novice to make his 4 points, himself taking the opportunity to throw off his worst hand (three Kings); or he might play his own best hand so as to at least divide the points. Throughout this version, each will be trying to estimate how much the other needs the points for the next round, and what he is likely to play. Opportunities for bluff are thereby introduced similar to those operating in the game of Gops (which is described in the next chapter).

Free hands. This is an extension of the above, in which not even the final playing hands are predetermined. Each player takes his 25 cards, makes a Poker hand, and plays the first round for 3 points as before. For the second round, each selects any five of his remaining cards and puts them face down on the table, both being turned when ready. In other words, the hands are made up as they go along. This considerably increases the skill factor, as both players must note which cards the other has not yet played and estimate their potential in combination.

Slow strip. This takes the element of bluff even further, and increases the scoring potential. It may be combined with any of the versions described above. At the start of every round, each player simultaneously reveals one card of his hand. If neither concedes defeat, a second is turned, and so on until one player concedes. Whoever wins the round, either because he has the better hand when all five are shown, or because the other concedes defeat earlier (in which case the unshown cards are rejected from play without being revealed) scores the value of the round multiplied by the number of cards he had revealed when conceded the win. Thus the first round may be worth anything from 3 to 15, and the last from 7 to 35.

15 GOPS

The origins of this unusual and unclassifiable game are unknown to me, so I shall plunge into it without further ado. It is a game of psychological warfare rather than mathematical analysis, and it is simple to learn and fast to play.

The game

Preliminaries. Divide the pack into four separate suits. Discard the hearts, which have no part to play, then shuffle the 13 diamonds and place them in a face down pile between both players. Each player then takes an entire black suit as his playing hand.

Object. The object is to capture the greatest value of diamonds, for which purpose each counts its face value from Ace = 1 to Ten = 10, then Jack 11, Queen 12 and King 13. As the total value of the diamond suit is 91, the player capturing 46 or more wins and no draw is possible.

Play Turn the top diamond face up to reveal its value and place it by the side of the stock. Each player then bids for it by choosing any one of his own (black) cards and laying it face down on the table before him. When both are ready, the two black cards are revealed. Whoever played the higher ranking card (Ace lowest, King highest) wins the diamond and places it face up on the table before him. The two black cards are now out of play for the rest of the game, but should be left face up so that each can see what the other has played and therefore, by deduction, know what he has left. The next diamond is then turned from the pack and played for in exactly the same way, and so on until all diamonds have been taken. If at any point both players play a card of the same rank, that result is a tie and the diamond remains untaken, though both black cards still count as spent and may not be taken back into hand. Then the next diamond is faced, and on this turn the winner takes both diamonds. If the result is still a tie, a third diamond is turned and the next winner takes all three, and so on.

Scoring. Each game is a separate event, but as it is boring to play any card game for a simple win/lose result the interest may be increased by crediting the winner with a score equivalent to the difference between the two totals captured (or with the number of points he has taken in excess of 45, which amounts to half the difference between the two).

Additional rules. I usually manage to resist the temptation to tinker about with established games, but all the published rules available to me seem deficient in one respect and rather flat in another.

First, what happens if there is a tie for the last diamond, together with any others that may have been tied in succession before it? The simplest solution is to credit it (them) to the player who made the immediately previous win. One of several alternative rules would be to leave them uncaptured, in which case a draw is possible; further, it might be agreed that if neither player captures a clear majority (46+) then the deal is a tie regardless of the amounts taken.

Second, one deal of Gops is too short to be considered a game in its own right: most players will want to go on playing it for a longer period. Yet if the two are evenly matched, there may only be a few points difference at the end of the whole game, which will seem too small to justify the amount of mental energy expended on the proceedings of the past hour or so. My suggestion for increasing the 'interest' of the relative scoring is one that I frequently apply to card games that score in ones and twos (especially Spite and Malice, of those in this book), and that is to expand the winner's score geometrically as follows:

	OVER 45:													
PTS TAKEN	1	2	3	4	5	6	7	8	9	10	11	12	13	etc
SCORE:	1	3	6	10	15	21	28	36	45	55	66	78	91	etc

Each successive score is found by adding the next appropriate number in the top row. For example, the score for taking 14 in excess of 45 is $91+14 = 105$, and so on. (If you would like it translated into algebra, the score for any given total n turns out to be $(n^2+n)/2$.) The net result is to give increasingly greater credit for taking increasingly greater totals, so that one player can win the whole game on one good result as opposed to a succession of mediocre ones.

It might also be agreed that the winner is the first player to reach a predetermined target score.

Suggestions for play

Gops is a game of bluff. If you want the next diamond from the stock, you will want to win it as cheaply as possible; if not, you will want your opponent to pay over the odds for it. A player wins cheaply when he captures a card by playing one that is only one or two ranks higher than his opponent's bid card, such as a Seven to a Six, because the latter will then have wasted 6/91 of his strength to no avail. An expensive win is made by the player who captures with, say, a King when his opponent has only played an Ace, for the former will then have paid a value of 11 over the odds for what he has purchased – *ie* he could have bought for 2 what he actually bought for 13. A cheap win is always worth having, no matter what the value of the diamond, but an expensive buy is even worse when the card bought is of comparatively low value – unless, of course, it is just enough to bring you over the 45 mark.

At each turn you both know how many diamonds the other has captured, and how much purchasing strength he has left. Play therefore consists in deciding how much you want the next diamond and how much you are prepared to pay for it, while at the same time estimating how much your opponent is prepared to bid. It is this question of estimating your opponent's strategy, and preventing him from divining your own, that makes Gops a game of players rather than a game of cards – in other words, a game of bluff.

As such, it admits of few guidelines to good play. The essence of most bluffing games is to avoid following the same strategy from game to game, for as soon as you become predictable, you will start being predicted, and to be predicted is to be pre-empted.

Suppose you start by deciding that you will pay for any card you want an amount equivalent to its value – an Ace for an Ace, Two for a Two, and so on. The first diamond turned is a Seven. As soon as your opponent has discovered your strategy, he will automatically play an Eight, thus winning a card of average value for a purchasing difference of one unit. To counter this, you might on the next identical occasion play a Nine, in the hope of overcoming his Eight by one unit and so getting a bargain buy. This time, however, he has predicted you – not by playing a Ten, and winning a Seven for a purchasing difference of one, but by playing his Ace, and making you win the Seven for a purchasing difference of eight – which is not what you had in mind at all!

At all times throughout the play you must bear in mind the relative number of diamond points captured by each of you to date, plus the relative purchasing power still available to each, and particularly the highest purchasing card left. Usually it is the player who is trailing who sets the pace. The one who has paid the greater price but at the same time bought an inferior aggregate cannot afford to waste his good cards on little diamonds. In this position he can only afford to concentrate on relative values, whereas the leading player has no money problems and can therefore direct the whole of his attention to divining his opponent's safest moves, and circumventing them.

Some of the thoughts that might occupy two players' attentions during the course of a deal could be illustrated from the following sample game.

1. *Seven of diamonds.* The card of exactly average value. Each player knows that to bid seven would be a waste, whether overtaken by the other's Eight or undercut by his Ace. Correctly foreseeing that Baker will play his Two for the best result against either manoeuvre, Abel wins it with his Three.

2. *Two.* Abel has more diamonds but Baker has marginally more cash. Neither is prepared to pay much for the Deuce, which in fact Abel wins by four to one. Now Abel is nine up, but has paid four more for that position.
3. *Four.* Baker cannot afford to let Abel win on lots of small diamonds, and ought to think about reducing the difference. To keep an edge on the resources, he can afford to pay perhaps three more than his estimate of what Abel is likely to offer for the Four. He therefore bids six, and very happily overcomes Abel's unexpected five. Now Abel is only five up in diamonds, and Baker three up in cash.
4. *Eight.* If Baker could win this, he would have 12 diamonds to Abel's nine. At this point he decides to have a flutter, playing the unexpectedly high Jack (worth 11, representing the value of the diamond under offer plus the amount of his cash surplus). But Abel anticipates such a move, and plays his Ace. Baker wins expensively, having now bought 12 for 20 as against Abel's nine for 10.
5. *Jack.* Now this is worth having – but how much is each prepared to pay for it? Abel must consider whether Baker will (a) try for it with his King or Queen, or (b) try to force Abel into an expensive win by undercutting with a low bid. Baker is unlikely to waste a card of middling value, which will probably be expensive whether a winner or a loser. He decides to let it go, playing his Two and leaving his hand with nothing lower than Six. Baker, foreseeing Abel's line of reasoning, in fact decided to play a middling card, the Seven, expecting Abel to have bid his Six. He therefore wins the Jack at a cost of five, and the situation now is: Abel 9 diamonds for 15, Baker 23 for 27, giving Baker the edge.
6. *Queen.* Abel, with more cash in hand, offers his Queen, feeling that Baker might play his King. As it happens, Baker followed the same line of thought and also played his Queen. Neither takes the diamond.
7. *King.* Now some hands are being forced: the winner of these two cards will net 25, and if it is Baker, he will have 48 and the game. Abel has no choice but to play his King, for if

this, too, is equalled, he can assuredly win the next turn with his Jack. Naturally, Baker plays his lowest card, the Three, leaving Abel with the 25 in diamonds at a difference in cost of 10 units. Situation so far: Abel has 34 for 38, Baker 23 for 42. A reversal of fortune: Abel is now much better off.

8. *Six*. There are 34 points-worth of diamonds left in play; here are six of them. Can Baker afford to make an expensive bid for this? Can he afford not to, as Abel will then be within six points of a win, and there are still the Nine and Ten to come with a Jack in Abel's hand? Again, Abel has no card lower than Six, but Baker has Four and Five to dispose of. There are several worse diamonds to throw them on, particularly the Ace and Three, which have yet to appear. Baker eventually bids with his Nine, and is gratified to beat Abel's Eight, after which the position is: Abel 34 for 46, Baker 29 for 51. Baker still trailing in both respects.
9. *Ten*. If Abel wins this, any succeeding diamond other than the Ace will give him the game. It is the highest of the diamonds left, and therefore justifies Baker's spending of his King on it. This being so, Abel can be expected to play a low card. In which case, Baker might risk playing his Ten. The danger is that Abel might overtake with the Jack. (A tie would be advantageous to Baker, who could then certainly win more on the next turn.) Baker decides to take that chance, and plays his Ten, Abel coming up with the Six. So far: Abel 34 for 52, with 7, 9, T, J in hand; Baker 39 for 61, with 4, 5, 8, K. This leaves A, 3, 5, 9 in the diamond stockpile. As the Nine will give him game, and Baker holds the highest card in play, he is bound to win.
10. *Five*. As this is the second best diamond left, Abel can afford to play his top card, the Jack. Nevertheless, he plays the Seven, trying to pull a fast one. If Baker anticipates the Jack by throwing his Four, Abel will win nine of the outstanding eighteen diamonds. Baker, however, foresees this manoeuvre, and plays his Eight.
11. *Ace*. Abel takes it. His cards are all as good as one another.
12. *Three*. Abel takes it.

13. *Nine.* Baker, having saved his King, takes the Nine. Result: Abel 38 diamonds, Baker 53 diamonds. That's eight points over the odds, which, by my scoring system, gives Baker 36 towards game. Had Abel's attempt to capture the Five cheaply succeeded, the game would have been 48 to 42, giving Baker only three over the odds for a game score of six.

Bluffing consists in doing the unexpected. This does not mean just doing the unusual or the speculative, because there are occasions on which such moves are expected, and therefore cannot amount to bluff. At move 9, above, Baker made a successful bluff by playing a middling card when common sense would have dictated the play of a high one. The bluff came off, and put him in a winning position. At move 10, Abel sought to reduce the score against him by playing lower than would appear sensible. But the bluff failed to work, because Baker expected it. And the reason why he expected it had nothing to do with mathematics or analysis or common sense. It was entirely due to the fact that Baker had played Abel before, and knew that he could nearly always be relied upon to play recklessly when his game was lost for certain.

16 CHALLENGE

This Russian game was introduced to the West in the early 1950s by Professor Besicovitch of Cambridge University, and seems first to have been published by Hubert Phillips under its present name. (Phillips gives the original as *Svoyi Koziri*, which may loosely be interpreted 'personal trumps'.) A Ukrainian lady has since drawn my attention to a similar game from her country called Durak (*ie* 'fool'), so we are evidently dealing with a peculiarly Slavic preference for chesslike games of calculation over cardlike games of chance and judgement. Chance enters into Challenge only to the extent that cards are shuffled and the opening positions consequently determined at random, but even this is balanced out by the fact that both players start with exactly equal opening positions and, throughout the game, have complete knowledge as to the lie of the cards in both hands. Like Chess, a game can go on for hours.

The game

Cards. Any short pack is used. Start with a 24-card pack (nothing lower than Nine), and, with growing expertise, increase the difficulty (and length) of play by using 28, 32 or even 36 cards. In the following account we will assume a 24-card pack, with cards ranking from high to low A K Q J T 9.

Trumps. A dealer having been chosen by any agreed method, he chooses any two suits to belong to himself and then nominates either one of them to be his personal trump suit. The other two suits belong to the non-dealer, and he similarly nominates one of them as his own trump. As there is no practical reason for preferring one suit to another at this stage, one might as well simplify matters by decreeing that the dealer's trump is spades and his plain suit diamonds, while his opponent's trump is hearts and his plain suit clubs. (Why bother to exercise freedom of choice if there is nothing worth exercising it on ?) Such, then, is the suit situation assumed in the following description.

Card distribution. Dealer now shuffles the pack thoroughly and deals out half of them (twelve) face up to the table. From these he rejects those of non-dealer's suits (hearts and clubs), and keeps those of his own (spades and diamonds) to form the basis of his playing hand. Now all the cards are revealed again, and non-dealer takes as the basis of his playing hand exactly the same cards in hearts as his opponent has in spades, and in clubs as his opponent in diamonds. Finally, those cards of the dealer's suits not held by himself are taken by non-dealer, and vice versa. The result is that each player's hand is an exact complement of the other's, each holding the same trumps, non-trumps, opposing trumps and opposing non-trumps as the other. For example:

	own tr	*own n-tr*	*opp tr*	*opp n-tr*
Dealer	♠K Q T	♢A J	♡A T 9	♣K Q T 9
Non-dealer	♡K Q T	♣A J	♠A T 9	♢K Q T 9

Object. To be the first to get rid of all one's cards.

Play. Non-dealer leads by playing any card face up to the table. Dealer must then either take it up into his own hand, or play a better card. A 'better card' is either a higher-ranking card of the suit led, or any card of one's personal trump suit. If he plays, non-dealer then has the same choice: either play a better card than dealer's, or take the cards so far played up into his own hand. Play continues in this way. So long as 'better' cards are played, cards played to the table remain on top of one another, slightly spread so that all are visible. Whenever a player is either unable or unwilling to play a better card than the previous one, he cannot play and must take the whole row of table cards and add them to his hand. The next lead is then made by the taker's opponent. The game ends as soon as one player plays his last card. That player is the winner.

Illustrative deal

Our players are Ivan and Nicholas. The hands are as given in the sample deal above, and, as Ivan dealt, Nicholas leads.

Nic	*Ivan*	*Nic*	*Ivan*	*Nic*	*Ivan*
♣J	♣K	♡9	♡T	Takes	◇Q (*note*)
♣A	♠Q	♡J	Takes	◇K	Takes
♠A	Takes	♡Q	♠K	♠9	♠K
♠9	♠T	♡A	Takes	Takes	◇K
♠J	♠Q	◇9	◇J	? ◇A	Takes and
Takes	♡9	◇Q	◇A		wins
♡J	♡A	♡K	Takes	◇T	◇J etc
Takes	♣9	◇K	◇A		

At the point of the first note, Ivan can win as soon as he has gained mastery in diamonds, for he has the best cards in all suits and has succeeded in seizing all Nicholas's personal trumps, without which the latter will have difficulty in getting back into play. The end became inevitable when Nicholas threw away his only top card, the Ace of diamonds, instead of taking in the King. After that, Ivan would capture any lead made by Nicholas (taking care to cover ◇T with the Jack, so as not to release a capturing card), then lead both black suits from the Ace downwards. Finally, he plays all his adversary's trumps (hearts) from the Ace down, allowing him no opportunity to capture. Of course, if he played hearts before either black suit, Nicholas would have taken in some of his own trumps and so been in a position to defend himself.

Notes on play

The illustrative deal is not an example of good play between experts, and I am not aware of any published material on the game – or even of any experts – to suggest that much study or practice has been devoted to discovering what good strategy might consist in. It is clear from the sample game, however, that a player who allows himself to lose all his trumps will be put very much on the defensive, and must at all costs endeavour to retain control of at least one plain suit – preferably his opponent's trump. The player who succeeds in capturing all the adverse trumps and holding top cards in other suits will win by playing them all from the top downwards, leaving his opponent's trump suit until last.

In case the question arises (though I think the rules are clear enough) it is not obligatory to follow suit to the previous card: you may trump or capture whether or not able to play a higher-ranking card of the suit led. It might also be noted that if you lead a card of your opponent's trump suit you considerably restrict his response, as he has but one suit to play from.

The sample game appended by the late Hubert Phillips to his description of Challenge in *The Pan Book of Card Games* assumes a method of play not followed in the above account. In his illustration, the game is played trick-wise – that is, the second player, having played a better card, then immediately leads any card of his choice, and so on. The method of play described here, in which cards are played alternately and each must be better than the last, is confirmed in another source, and I think it makes for a better game than the trick method. You may like to try both and see if you agree.

17 MATE

This game was invented by a German, G. Capellen, and first published in 1915. It was rescued from oblivion by the American game-researcher Sid Sackson in his book *A Gamut of Games*, of which the British edition first appeared in 1974. Mate, as Sackson observes, is 'a game that, through unfortunate circumstances, was doomed to an untimely death, but one that eminently deserves to be revived. It is played with only twenty cards. Yet with this limited material an amazing diversity of playing situations develop. And it is, almost unique among card games, completely a game of skill'.

The game

Cards. Twenty, consisting of the Ace, Ten, King, Queen and Seven of each suit. (This constitutes the single Mate pack. A double Mate pack for advanced players is described at the end of this chapter, along with several variations in play.)

Deal. Shuffle the cards thoroughly and deal ten to each player in two batches of five.

Object. To be the last to play a card. Each in turn plays a card to the table in accordance with rules of sequence described below. As soon as one player cannot legally follow the previous card he is 'mated'. His opponent then gets a score based on the value of the card with which he delivered mate, and the number of cards already played.

Rank and value of cards. Within each suit, cards rank from high to low A T K Q 7, and bear point-values which are respectively 11, 10, 4, 3 and 7. As between suits, clubs are highest, followed by spades, hearts, and finally diamonds. In a sense, then, ♣A is the highest card in the pack and ♢7 the lowest. A diagram may clarify this schedule:

♣	A	T	K	Q	7
♠	A	T	K	Q	7
♡	A	T	K	Q	7
◇	A	T	K	Q	7
value:	*11*	*10*	*4*	*3*	*7*

Play. Non-dealer leads by playing any card face up to the table before him. Dealer responds by playing any card of the same suit on the table before him, keeping it separate from his opponent's. Whoever plays the higher ranking card leads to the second turn, and so on. If at any turn the second player has no card of the suit led, he must instead play a card of the same rank. In this event the player of the higher suit leads to the next turn. If the second player cannot match the lead by suit or by rank, he is mated and the deal ends. Do not yet mix all the cards up.

Score. The player of the last card now records a score consisting of (a) the value of the last card he played, *multiplied by* (b) the number of the turn on which he delivered mate. Thus if non-dealer led ♠Q and dealer had no Queen or spade with which to follow, the leader would score 3×1 (Queen × first turn) = 3, the lowest possible. At the other extreme, a player delivering mate with an Ace on the tenth and last turn would score $11 \times 10 = 110$.

Game. When the first deal has been played and scored, each player picks up the cards he has played, adds them to those remaining in his hand, and exchanges them for those of his opponent. Now a second round is played and scored, exactly as before except with the hands reversed so that neither player has had the advantage of better cards – or rather, both have had the same advantage. The first lead is made from the same hand as before, but of course by the player who originally dealt. After this round has been played, the cards are gathered up, shuffled, and redealt by the other player. Two more rounds are played in the same way, with hands swapped over as before, and scores are added to determine the final result.

Notes on play

The purpose of swapping hands is to ensure that both players will have made use of the same resources, so that whoever plays better scores more. At least, that's the theory, though it might be held that the second player of the leading hand is in a position to observe the outcome of his opponent's play and either avoid what proved to be weak lines or make improvements to good ones. The playing of a second deal (two more rounds) redresses the balance.

The game as described above is not complete, and an extension of the rules is given at the end of this section. Even so, it is enough to be starting with. At beginners' Stage I it will be sufficient to concentrate on playing the last card. At Stage II you will seek to play in such a way as to make the highest score. The extension referred to later may be regarded as Stage III.

Here are one or two observations that may be made about the different stages.

STAGE ONE: If the cards are fairly evenly divided, with both players holding at least one of each rank and two of each suit, be prepared for a fairly long and intricate game. If, however, there is a marked imbalance, the chances are that the leading hand has a calculable win, and if the first leader muffs it, his opponent may profit from the mistake by avoiding it.

Try to visualise the way in which both hands interlock, perhaps in some such way as illustrated in Figure 6. The process of play may then, if it helps, be translated into terms of a board game.

It is nearly always advantageous to lead to a turn, as you then choose the next point of attack. It is therefore desirable to play the better card at each turn, if this can be done without spoiling the hand.

Try to keep back at least one card of each suit and one of each rank, as you cannot be mated so long as you succeed in doing this. Conversely, concentrate on ridding your opponent of his shortest suit as soon as possible, and play from three of a kind (*ie* three Aces or whatever) when you can.

STAGE TWO: At Stage II, which may be subtitled 'Playing to the Score', get rid of your Kings and Queens first if you are confident of winning, whether because of the cards you hold or because you consider yourself the better player. You can then expect to win with a card of high value for a high-scoring game. Your score will also be higher if you can keep the game open as long as possible, so that more turns will have been played. Conversely, if you have little expectation of winning, try to force an early end to the play. In this event it does not matter what value of cards you hold or play, as they will not affect your opponent's score.

Before describing extensions of the game, I must mention in passing that anyone who knows Germany's national card game, Skat, will recognise some of its influences on the structure of the game. For instance, the order of suits from clubs high to diamonds low comes from Skat, as do the relative ranking of the cards within in each suit and the point-values 11, 10, 4 and 3 for Ace, Ten, King and Queen. (In counting 7 for the Seven, notice how Capellen has picked on a value exactly mid-way between the Ace-Ten and King-Queen averages.) Also characteristic of Skat is the practice of dealing ten cards each in two batches of five – once widely followed though not now officially approved – and even the device of multiplying values to determine a final score. It is fascinating to speculate on how the game would have emerged had the same idea been worked up by an English player of Crib, an American of Poker, or a French of Belote!

Variants

Foreplacing and overmate. When you have played the basic form of the game as described above, you will be ready for the additional feature of 'foreplacing', as follows.

After the deal or exchange, but before the first lead, either or both players may select one card from their hand and put it face down to one side, where it remains out of play for the whole round. The effect of doing so is to increase the winner's score by adding one multiplier to the number of turns, so that, for example, a win on the seventh move multiplies by eight instead of seven. It is clear that you will foreplace if you are confident of winning, so as to boost your own score.

It may be necessary to add that the 'turn factor' is increased by one only, whether one or both players foreplace. But an interesting situation arises if only one player foreplaces, so that he is playing with only nine cards as against his opponent's ten. In this event, the player with only nine cards will, if he gets as far as the tenth move, pick up the card he played on his ninth turn and use it again as his tenth – if, of course, it will follow. If now either player wins on the tenth move, he has given 'over-mate' and scores double. For example, if overmate is given with an Ace on the tenth move, it scores $11 \times 11 \times 2 = 242$, which is the highest possible in the game.

Several other rule variants exist which might be adopted by agreement, being offered for what is described as 'a change of pace'. In my view they do not add much to a game that is already full of riches in its most basic form.

Free move. At any point during the course of play, either player (but only one, and whichever of them happens to use it first) may refrain from following suit even though able, and instead play a card of the same rank.

King's privilege. By this rule, the lead of a King must be followed by another King if possible; if not, suit is followed instead.

Court privilege. Same as King's privilege, but applying to Queens as well. Either version may, by agreement, be combined with the free move rule described above.

Double Mate. This version is played without any Queens, but with the addition of certain doubled cards as follows: ♢A, ♡T, ♠K, ♣7, restoring the pack to twenty. It introduces considerable subtlety to the game, unlike the cheap frills described above.

Self-mate. In this version, proposed by the present author, the first multiplier is the value of the mating card (as before) but the second, instead of being the turn number, is the value of the last card played by the loser. The lowest winning score is therefore $3 \times 3 = 9$ and the highest $11 \times 11 = 121$. If one foreplaces, the winner's score is doubled (maximum 242); if both foreplace, it is trebled (363); and a win by overmate is quadrupled (484).

Illustrative deal

The cards are dealt as follows:

Dr Jekyll ♣...Q7 ♠....7 ♡.TK.. ◇ATKQ7
Mr Hyde ♣ATK.. ♠ATKQ. ♡A..Q7 ◇.....

Mr Hyde can see an easy way to win, taking advantage of Jekyll's weakness in spades and Aces by voiding him of both and then leading ♠A. He does this by leading ♠Q to draw the Seven, then ♣A to draw the ◇A, then ♠A to leave his opponent no saving move. He scores 33, winning with an Ace (11) on the third move.

Now hands are exchanged and Dr Jekyll shows how to make proper use of the hand. He starts by foreplacing ♠K, and the game proceeds thus:

Turn no.	1	2	3	4	5	6	7	8	9	10
Jekyll	♣K	♣A	♣T	♠Q	♠T	♡A	♡Q	♡7	♠A	♠A
Hyde	♣Q	♣7	◇T	♠7	♡T	♡K	◇Q	◇7	◇A	?

Having foreplaced, Jekyll uses his ninth card as his tenth, leaving Hyde unable to play his ◇K, and wins by overmate. His score is 11 for the Ace, times 11 for winning on the tenth move in a foreplaced game, times 2 for overmate, total 242.

FIGURE 6

It may help to visualise one's hand of cards in a pattern of this sort, bearing in mind that the blanks represent cards held by one's opponent. The lowest cards are at the bottom and on the right, the highest at the top and on the left. Tricks may be thought of as moves on a game-board looking like this. The hand shown here is one of those used in the illustrative deal.

18 ABSTRAC

This game, one of my own invention, is an adaptation for playing cards of a well-known family of games called Nim. In particular, it is most like the Matchsticks Game in which thirteen matches are laid in a row, each player in turn taking one, two or three matches away, and the one who captures the last match is the winner (or the loser, depending on which has been agreed). Like Noughts and Crosses, the Matchsticks Game has an easily discoverable 'best' way of playing, and the game loses its interest once you have discovered it. In Abstrac, however, there is considerably more variety . . . as you will see.

The game

Cards. Twenty four, using only the A K Q J T and 9 of each suit.

Deal. Shuffle thoroughly and then lay the cards face up in a row on the table between the two players. Cards may overlap to save space, but all must be identifiable from their edges.

Object. The object is twofold: (a) to capture sets of three or four cards of the same rank, and sequences of three or more cards in the same suit; but at the same time (b) to avoid capturing any cards you do not need for such combinations, as there is a penalty for taking more than 12 of the 24 cards. Excess cards are safe if they form combinations, but costly if they are unrelated.

Play. Each player in turn takes one, two or three consecutive cards from the top end of the layout and places them face up on the table before him. (The top end is the one with the uncovered card – see diagram.) It is for non-dealer to make the first capture, but he may pass the lead to his opponent if he thinks it advantageous to do so. Thereafter each plays in turn and neither may pass. Captured cards must remain open on the table, and should be arranged by rank and suit so that at any given point each player can see exactly how his opponent is faring. Play continues until all cards have been captured.

Score. There are two parts to the scoring, in accordance with the twofold object of the game. The first is for combinations and the second is for cards.

(*a*) *Combinations* A set is three or four cards of the same rank, a sequence three or more cards of the same suit running in the following order: A K Q J T 9. Any card may be counted as both part of a sequence and part of a set. The scores are:

Set of three	2
Set of four	8
Sequence of three	3
Sequence of four	4
Sequence of five	6
Sequence of six	12

(*b*) *Cards* Each player now takes his total score for combinations and multiplies this by the number of cards captured by his opponent. Thus if both players take twelve each, the multipliers will be the same and the game will be decided, in effect, on combinations alone. If, however, both have scored the same for combinations but have taken different numbers of cards, then the player who took the fewer cards will win.

Game. A game should consist of several deals, each dealing alternately, and the winner is the player first to reach a previously agreed target – say 300 for a short game.

Suggestions for play

If your opponent dealt, make the first move if you can see good purpose in doing so, but pass it if not, so that dealer will have problems to sort out for himself. What constitutes good purpose in doing so is not easy to explain, because it really depends on how far ahead you can calculate. In theory, any given order of cards must permit of a forced win for either the player who moves first or the one who moves second, assuming that both play 'perfectly'.

As non-dealer has the choice of moving first or second, he always has a theoretical forced win (or, at worst, a draw). Therefore, in principle, the decision whether to play first or pass the lead is one on which success or failure depends absolutely. But all this is highly theoretical, as hardly any player in real life can be expected to have the powers of analysis sufficiently well developed to play perfectly. The further ahead you can see, the more you will win. If you can see nothing to be gained by starting, pass the lead.

As a matter of general strategy, you will naturally try to make sets of four and sequences of six (*ie*, entire suits), though you will rarely succeed because your opponent need take only a few specific cards to render that objective unattainable. The defensive side of this coin is to ensure that you do not allow him any quartet or sequence of six; you prevent these by endeavouring to capture at least one card of each rank and one card of each suit. Any card of one rank will do to stop the quartet, but the ideal cards to take in prevention of long sequences are Jacks and Queens, as they restrict runs to only three, namely A–K–Q if the Jack is taken, or J–T–9 if the Queen. At each turn, therefore, always stop to consider which cards you still lack to prevent your opponent from making high-scoring combinations, and play in such a way as to capture them either now or later.

If at any point in the game you are in doubt as to how many cards to take, take only one. If you cannot win on combinations, you may win on cards by taking fewer of them.

Now we come to the fundamental tactic of the game, which you would soon discover for yourself even if it were not drawn to your attention. When it is your turn to play, you can always play in such a way as to capture any one of three desired cards on your *following* turn – or, what comes to the same thing, to prevent your opponent from taking any one of them on his own immediate turn.

Consider the layout illustrated. If the leader takes only one card, the ♢T, then he can also take the fourth card along from it, the ♡K, no matter whether his opponent takes one, two or three cards. If he takes the first two, he also forces the fourth along from ♡T, namely ◇K; similarly, by taking the first three, he secures access to ◇J. Whether he will take one, two or three may therefore depend on which (if any) of the cards ◇A, ♡K, ◇K he may want in addition – or may wish to deny his opponent.

The same principle can be taken even further, for as many steps as you wish. By removing just the first card in this layout (◇T), the leader could also, if they were of use to him, take not only the fourth away (♡K) but also the eighth (♣9), twelfth (◇Q), sixteenth (♠K) and twentieth (♡9). If those particular cards happened to be all of a suit, this is the strategy he would adopt. (To combat this, his opponent would take only one card at each turn, finishing up with a multiplier of 17 as against leader's 7.)

Illustrative deal

Let's look at the illustrated diagram, and see how the game might proceed. Our players are Alpha and Beta.

First, Alpha must decide whether to play or pass. A good move might be to take the first three, winning a pair of Tens and securing, by the rule of four, the ◇J to go with the ◇T and ♠J. If Beta then took the pair of Kings, he (Alpha) would gain a third Jack to boot. But Beta might instead follow the strategy of taking only one card at a time, which would give Alpha too many. He contents himself with taking the pair of Tens only, denying Beta the pair of Kings.

Beta takes just the ♠J, allowing Alpha another pair (in itself useless) but denying him the useful ◇J, and giving himself the advantage of fewer cards.

Alpha next takes three, including the pair of Kings, on the principle that if he is going to take more cards he may as well make as many combinations as possible.

Beta then takes the pair of Jacks, giving himself a highly economical three-card hand worth two points already, and, as they are all Jacks, preventing Alpha from making long runs in three suits. By the rule of four, he can also force the other Jack, increasing his score by 8 points.

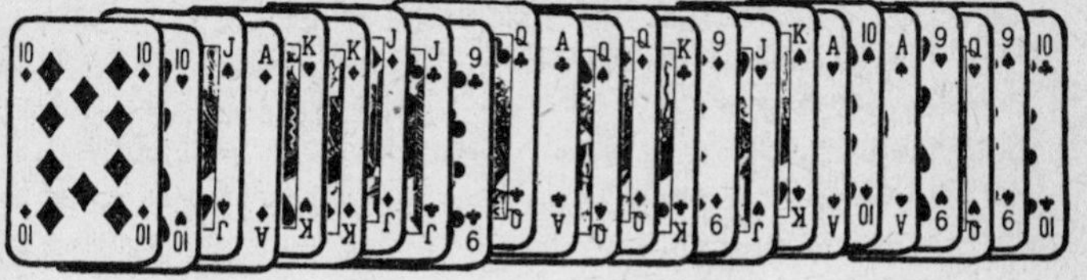

FIGURE 7

The layout of cards at the start of the game discussed in the text. There are over one and a quarter million different ways in which the game might proceed, and millions more different ways in which the cards may be arranged in the first place.

Next available to Alpha are three unconnected clubs, which are useless to himself and not much better for Beta. He takes just ♣9.

To force the ♡J, Beta should now take ♣Q, ♣A and ♠Q. But for better or for worse – and you can work out which for yourself – he prefers not to take so many useless cards and contents himself with ♣Q alone.

Alpha cannot now take ◇Q to add to his King and Ace, otherwise he gives Beta the fourth Jack. He therefore takes two, giving himself ♠Q to guard against Queens and spades in the other hand, and reserving ♡J to himself.

Beta takes ♣K to go with his Ace, Queen and Jack, along with ◇Q. He leaves ◇9, as it is of no real use to either player, and in any case to deny Alpha the ♡A.

Alpha must take ◇9 and the Jack wanted by his opponent, but has no use for ♠K.

Beta takes the next three cards and Alpha the three after that, both for reasons that will be obvious if you are following it through, and Beta has the last two, giving him a total of 11 cards against Alpha's 13.

For combinations, Alpha has a sequence of five hearts to the King, worth 6, plus 2 each for the trio of Aces and Nines, 10 in all. Multiplying by the number of cards taken by his opponent, he finishes with a score of 110.

Beta has sequences of three spades and four clubs for 7, plus 2 for his Jacks, making 9. Multiplying by Alpha's cards, he finishes with a score of 117. The results are about average, though unusually close.

To show that such results are not a foregone conclusion, it will be interesting to see what would have happened had the same layout of cards been played in another way.

If both players had automatically taken three cards at each turn, the leader would have scored 120 and so would dealer – a tie. If they had each taken two per turn, leader would have finished with 144 to 84 – a difference of 60. If they had taken one each alternately, leader would have scored 204 to 120 – a difference of 64. In trying other possible ways of playing the same cards, you may like to note in passing that there are over 1¼ *million* different ways in which any single arrangement of cards could be played, while the number of significantly different ways in which the cards can be arranged to start with amounts to 34×10^{27} (that is, 34 followed by 27 noughts).

Variants

There are several interesting ways in which the basic rules can be varied. If you play with a 36-card pack, adding the Eights, Sevens and Sixes, the scores are as follows:

Set of three	3
Set of four	12
Sequence of three	3
Sequence of four	4
Sequence of five	5
Sequence of six	6
Sequence of seven	10
Sequence of eight	15
Sequence of nine	25

Instead of using the combinations described in the basic game, you may prefer to score for making Poker hands, or melds from other favourite games such as Pinochle, Bézique, Cribbage or Cassino.

GLOSSARY OF TERMS

Adverse Belonging to one's opponent.

Bézique The ♠Q and ◇J together.

Box At Cribbage, the dealer is 'in the box' by virtue of owning the crib (which itself comes from a word meaning 'box' or 'container').

Build At Cassino, a group of cards that must be taken as a whole, not individually; or, to make such a build by putting cards together.

Capot At Piquet, the winning of all twelve tricks. (The stress is on the second syllable, and the T not pronounced.)

Court cards Kings, Queens and Jacks.

Deadwood At Gin Rummy, cards left in hand that cannot form melds or be laid off against them.

Declare To announce and score for a valid combination of cards.

Deuce The Two of any suit.

Discard To reject cards from the hand. Also, to play to a trick a card which is neither of the suit led nor a trump.

Draw To take a card from the pack.

Elder The player who leads or otherwise makes the first move of a game; usually the non-dealer.

Flush A hand of cards all of the same suit.

Follow suit. To play a card of the same suit as the one that was led.

Fours or Four of a Kind: a Poker hand consisting of four cards of the same rank plus any one other.

Full house A Poker hand consisting of three cards of one rank and two of another.

Game Period of play, consisting of as many deals as may be agreed or fixed by the rules, after which accounts are settled. Or, a predetermined target score whose attainment by either player ends the period of play known as the game, in which case a game is defined as '500 up' (or whatever the target may be). For specialised meaning at All Fours, see page 27.

Gin A hand containing all melds and no deadwood.

Guard A player's highest card in a given suit is 'guarded' if he holds as many cards of that suit below it as his opponent holds above it.

High At All Fours, the highest trump in play.

His heels, his nob At Cribbage, dealer scores 'two for his heels' if he turns a Jack as the start, and either player 'one for his nob' if he holds the Jack of the same suit as the start.

Lead To play the first card to a trick.

Low At All Fours, the lowest trump in play.

Marriage King and Queen of the same suit, in games where this is a scoring feature.

Meld At Rummy, three or more cards of the same rank, or of the same suit and in numerical sequence.

Pair Two cards of the same rank (accompanied, in Poker hands, by three unrelated cards).

Peg At Cribbage, to mark a score by pegging it on the Cribbage board.

Plain suit Any suit other than trumps.

Point At Piquet, the highest value of cards in one suit held by either player.

Prial At Cribbage, three cards of the same rank; a corruption of 'pair royal'.

Quatorze At Piquet, four cards of the same rank, not lower than Tens.

Quint At Piquet, five cards in suit and sequence.

Rank The denomination of a card – e.g. Ace, King, Two, Three and so on.

Revoke To fail to follow suit to the card led although able to do so and required by the rules to do so.

Run At Cribbage, three or more cards in numerical sequence, e.g. 9–T–J, regardless of suit.

Sequence Three or more cards of the same suit and in numerical sequence, at Piquet or Bézique, for example.

Singleton A holding of only one card in any given suit.

Start At Cribbage, the top card of the stock turned up at the start of play.

Stock Undealt cards placed face down at the start of play.

Straight Poker hand consisting of five cards in numerical sequence.

Talon At Piquet, the stock.

Tenace A holding of the first and third, or second and fourth, best cards of a given suit.

Tenth At Cribbage, a card worth 10 (T, J, Q or K).

Threes or *Three of a Kind:* a Poker hand consisting of three cards of the same rank and two odd ones.

Trick See 'Notes to Text', p xi.

Trump The superior suit. See p xi.

Two Pair A Poker hand consisting of two pairs and one odd card.

Unguarded In one player's hand, the highest card of a given suit is unguarded if his opponent cannot fail to capture it by leading from the top downwards in that suit. See also 'guard'..

Upcard Top card of the waste or discard pile at Gin Rummy.

Void The holding of no cards in a given suit.

Waste Pile Pile made by discards at Gin Rummy.

Younger The opposite of elder (see entry); therefore, usually, the dealer.

GAME SUMMARIES

PART ONE: GAMES WITH A FULL PACK

Cribbage (pages 3–16)

Deal. Five or six cards each; discard two to dealer's crib; non-dealer cuts and dealer turns 'start' card.

Scores.

3 for last to non-dealer (Five-card only)
2 for his heels to dealer for turning Jack
2 per fifteen in hand, crib or play
2 per pair in hand, crib or play
6 per prial in hand, crib or play
12 per double prial in hand, crib or play
1 *per card* in run of 3+ in hand, crib or play
1 *per card* of flush in hand, in hand plus start, or in crib plus start (but not in play)
1 for his nob (Jack of same suit as start) in hand or crib
1 for a go in play
2 for making up thirty-one in play

Game. If 61 up (usual for Five-card), 31 saves the lurch or double loss; if 121 (usual for Six-card) the lurch is 91; if 181, lurch is 121.

Optional rules. Lurch, muggins.

Gin Rummy (pages 17–25)

Deal. Ten each one at a time; form stock and upcard.

Start. Non-dealer may start by taking upcard; if not, dealer may start by taking upcard; if not, non-dealer must start by drawing from stock.

Knocking. Knock with 10 or less. (Variant: Value of first upcard determines maximum value for knocking; if an Ace, knock only on a gin hand.) Opponent of knocker may lay off against knocker's melds unless knocker went gin.

Scores

(*a*) If knocker has lower count, difference in deadwood, plus 25 if gin.

(*b*) If opponent has equal or lower, difference plus 25 for undercut but nothing for gin.

(*c*) Game is 100 up. Add:
100 for winning
25 per won hand (box bonus)
100 plus twice basic score for winning all hands (shutout bonus)

NOTE: Last two cards of stock may not be taken. No-score draw if reached.

All Fours (pages 26–31)

Deal. Six each in threes; turn card for proposed trump. If not accepted, 'run cards' by dealing three more each and turning another; and so on until accepted. Then reduce hands to six before play.

Play. Non-dealer always leads. Either follow suit or trump, as preferred, but play nothing else unless unable to follow.

Scores. One point each for:
Turning a Jack (unless that suit already refused).
Gift, to non-dealer if dealer accepts trump.
High: being dealt highest trump in play.
Low: being dealt (or capturing) lowest trump in play.
Jack: capturing Jack of trumps if in play.
Game: capturing higher value of cards, counting each Ace 4, King 3, Queen 2, Jack 1, Ten 10. No score if tied.

Game. Either 11 points (original) or 7 (modern).

Variants. In All Fives, score also 4 for capturing Ace of trumps, King 3, Queen 2, Jack 1, Ten 10, Five 5 (and count trump Five as 5 when counting for 'game' point). Game is 61 up; score on a Cribbage board. In Pitch, higher bidder leads and that card determines trumps.

Cassino (pages 35–40)

Deal. Four each and to the table in twos. Deal four more each when cards played out.

Value. Cards count face value, with Ace 1, but courts no value.

Play. Options at each turn:

(*a*) Capture by pairing or totalling, but courts only by pairing and only one at a time.
(*b*) Build pairs or totals for subsequent capture, provided that you can do so.
(*c*) Increase such builds, provided that you can capture.
(*d*) Trail, unless you can capture a build you previously made or increased.

Scores.

3 for majority of cards
1 per majority of spades
2 for ♢T, Big Cassino
1 for ♠2, Little Cassino
1 per Ace
1 per sweep

Variant: Royal Cassino. Jack 11, Queen 12, King 13, Ace 1 or 14.

Variant: Spade Cassino. Instead of 1 for majority of spades, score 2 each for Ace, Two and Jack, 1 for each other spade.

Spite and Malice (pages 41–50)

Deal. Five each from the pack with four Jokers, 26 each from the other pack to form two private stocks. Upturn private stock card: higher rank starts.

Play. Build centre stacks from Ace to King regardless of suit. Top card of private pack is only playable to the centre – Ace or Two must be played if possible, other ranks optional. Cards from hand may be played to centre or to one of four waste piles. A card may be played to the top of a waste pile if it is equal in rank to, or one lower than, the previous card. The top card of a waste pile is always available for play to a centre stack. Jokers are wild throughout. Cards may not be played to or from opponent's stock or waste piles. For playing all five cards from hand, have another turn.

Re-starting. Shuffle completed centre stacks into main stockpile whenever one contains 12 or fewer cards. If none completed, shuffle all incomplete stacks in. If neither player can or will go, gather all cards except private stocks, shuffle thoroughly and start again from scratch.

PART TWO: GAMES WITH A SHORT PACK

Piquet (pages 53–77)

Cards. 32, ranking A K Q J T 9 8 7 in all suits. No trump.

Preliminary. Game is six deals. Higher cut chooses whether or not to deal first. Deal 12 each in twos or threes. Spread remaining eight face down. After checking for carte blanche, elder must discard and draw from one to five cards, then younger from one to as many as are left.

Play. Elder declares first, in order carte blanche (if applicable), point, sequence, then set. Elder leads; younger scores for any valid declarations and then follows. All declarations scored for must be identified, if not shown. Normal rules of trick play at no trump.

Scores.

10 for carte blanche (no courts): must be proved.

1 per card of best point suit: superiority of holdings determined by counting each Ace 11, court 10, others face value.

1 per card of best sequence of three or more, plus 10 if five or more.

3 per trio of any rank higher than Nine.

14 per quatorze of any rank higher than Nine.

60 for repique, *ie* counting 30 in declarations before opponent scores and any card is led.
30 for pique, *ie* counting 30 in declarations and tricks before opponent scores.
1 to elder for leading, as of right.
1 for winning a trick led by oneself.
2 for winning a trick led by one's opponent.
10 for winning a majority of tricks, PLUS
30 (40 in all) for capot – winning all twelve.

NOTE: Only one player may score for point, sequence or trio/quatorze. Neither scores if neither has a better point or sequence than the other, but whoever has the best sequence or trio/quatorze may score for any others of the same type.

Game score. 100 plus difference between two totals. If loser fails to reach rubicon of 100, winner scores 100 plus *total* of two game scores (even if rubiconed himself). In the event of a tie, play two more deals.

Sixty Six (97–101)

Cards.	Rank:	A	T	K	Q	J	9
	Value:	11	10	4	3	2	0

Deal. Six each in twos, and turn up trumps.

Tricks. Follow suit, trump or discard *ad lib*; draw from stock to restore hand to six cards. Having won a trick, declare a trump marriage for 40 or common marriage for 20 by leading either card from it. Nine of trumps may be exchanged for turn-up. After stock exhausted, must follow suit if possible and win the trick if possible. Twelfth trick scores 10. Declare 'out' upon reaching 66 points. If right, score 1 game point, or 2 if opponent has not reached 33 (*schneider*), or 3 if opponent has taken none (*schwarz*). If wrong, opponent scores 2, or 3 if he has taken no tricks.

Foreclosing. Either player may foreclose by turning down the trump card, and the last six tricks are played immediately without scoring 10 for last.

Bézique (pages 53–77)

Table of scores: The sign (–) means 'not applicable'.

	One pack	Two pack	Four pack	Six pack	Eight pack
Deal to each	8	8	9	12	15
Carte blanche	—	—	50	250	—
SEQUENCES					
Trump (A T K Q J)	150	250	250	250	250
Plain (A T K Q J)	—	—	150	150	150
Royal marriage	40	40	40	40	40
Common marriage	20	20	20	20	20
QUARTETS, QUINTETS					
Any four Aces	100	100	100	100	100
Any four Kings	80	80	80	80	80
Any four Queens	60	60	60	60	60
Any four Jacks	40	40	40	40	40
Four trump Aces	—	—	—	1000	1000
Four trump Tens	—	—	—	900	900
Four trump Kings	—	—	—	800	800
Four trump Queens	—	—	—	600	600
Four trump Jacks	—	—	—	400	400
Five trump Aces	—	—	—	—	2000
Five trump Tens	—	—	—	—	1800
Five trump Kings	—	—	—	—	1600
Five trump Queens	—	—	—	—	1200
Five trump Jacks	—	—	—	—	800
BEZIQUES					
Bézique (or binocle): ♠Q–♢J‡	40	40	40	40	40
Double bézique	—	500	500	500	500
Triple bézique	—	—	1500	1500	1500
Quadruple bézique	—	—	—	4500	4500
Quintuple bézique	—	—	—	—	9000
Grand binocle: ♠K–♠Q–♢J	80	—	—	—	—

‡ *Suits variable in some forms of the game – see full account.*

	One pack	Two pack	Four pack	Six pack	Eight pack
OTHER FACTORS					
Declaring trump Seven (X = may be exchanged with turn-up)	10	10X	—	—	—
Winning last trick	10	10	50	250	250
Game bonus	—	—	500	1000	1000
Rubicon bonus	—	d'ble	500	loser's total	

In Two-pack, brisques (Aces and Tens) count 10 each captured in tricks; in Four-pack, they are counted only to break a tie. In One-pack (Binocle) each captured Ace scores 11, Ten 10, King 4, Queen 3, Jack 2.

Klabberjass (pages 102–111)

Deal. Six each in threes, turn next card for trump proposal.

Bids. Starting with non-dealer, each may accept the trump suit turned, or schmeiss (offer either acceptance or fresh deal), or pass. After two passes, either nominate another suit or pass. After two more passes, throw hands in. Trumps established, non-dealer leads. Trump seven may be exchanged for turn-up if same suit.

Tricks. If trumps led, follower must win if possible; if unable to follow plain suit lead, follower must trump if possible.

Rank	Jass	Menel	A	T	K	Q	J	9	8	7
Value	20	14	11	10	4	3	2	0	0	0

Jass = trump Jack *Menel* = trump Nine

Other scores. As to sequences, only the player with the best scores, and he scores any others he may hold. For this purpose only, cards rank A K Q J T 9 8 7.

Sequence of three	= 20	declare before tricks
Sequence of more	= 50	
Bella (K+Q trumps)	= 20	declare by leading from
Stich (last trick)	= 10	

Score. Game is 500 up. Each scores as made, but if bidder fails to take more than opponent (bête), the latter scores the points made by both. If final scores are equal, bidder is half-bête and merely scores nothing.

Ecarté (pages 112–121)

Cards. Rank: K Q J A T 9 8 7.

Deal. Five each, turn next for trump.

Play. When elder ceases to propose new cards or younger ceases to accept proposal.

Tricks. Second to play must always follow suit if possible and always win the trick if possible.

Score.
1 for turning the trump King, or declaring it.
1 for the point (three or four tricks).
2 for the vole (all five tricks).
2 for winning (3–5 tricks) if opponent played without proposing, or refused a first proposal.

Game is 5 up.

Le Truc (pages 122–126)

Cards. Rank: 7 8 A K Q J T 9.

Deal. Three each. Non-dealer may propose one fresh deal, which younger may accept or refuse.

Tricks. No need to follow suit. Trick won by higher-ranking card. If equal, trick tied.

Object. Win two tricks, a tied trick going to the first player to win a trick.

Double. Either may double before playing a card (except the first lead): if accepted, the game value is doubled and played on; if not, the game value is not doubled but the doubler wins. Do not double beyond amount needed for game (12 points): instead, bid 'Remainder'. Opponent may refuse or bid his own remainder.

PART THREE: GAMES OF EQUAL OPPORTUNITY

Poker Squares and Quintet (pages 129–140)

Relative status of Poker hands at Quintet	Score at Poker Squares	Explanation of Poker hand
straight flush	30	five in suit and sequence
four of a kind	16	four of same rank
full house	10	three-kind plus pair
flush	5	five same suit
straight	12	five in sequence
three of a kind	6	three of same rank
two pair	3	two each of two ranks
one pair	1	two of same rank
nothing	0	none of the above

Between hands containing no combination, the one with the highest card wins, second highest if equal, and so on.

Poker Squares. One player draws 25 cards one at a time and builds a Poker square as he does so. Opponent extracts same cards from his pack and does likewise. Player building higher valued square wins, counting appropriate score for each row and column.

Quintet. Remove seven cards at random from 32-card pack. Each arranges identical 25-card pack in five Poker hands. Winner of first hand scores 3, second 4, third 5, fourth 6, fifth 7. Divide equally if tied.

Gops – see pages 141–147

Challenge – see pages 148–151

Mate (pages 152–158)

Rank and value of cards

♣	A	T	K	Q	7	These suits are
♠	A	T	K	Q	7	listed in order of
♡	A	T	K	Q	7	seniority: *ie* Clubs
◇	A	T	K	Q	7	is the highest and
Values:	*11*	*10*	*4*	*3*	*7*	diamonds the lowest.

Deal. Ten each in fives. Non-dealer leads.

Player. Follower must play a card of the same suit if possible; if not, a card of the same rank if possible; if not, he loses. Player of higher rank (or higher suit, as case may be) leads to the next move.

Score. Last to play scores value of card played multiplied by number of move on which he won.

Abstrac (pages 159–164)

Deal. 24 cards face up in a row, overlapping. Leader may play or pass the lead.

Play. At each turn take one, two or three cards from top end of spread.

Score. For combinations to be made from cards taken as follows:

Sequence of three	3
Sequence of four	4
Sequence of five	6
Sequence of six	12
Set of three	2
Set of four	8

A card may form part of a sequence and part of a set. For sequence, cards run A K Q J T 9.

Game score. Each player totals his score for combinations and multiplies this by the number of cards taken by his opponent.

CHESS

GERALD ABRAHAMS

Clear and stimulating, this guide to chess provides a thorough explanation and analysis of the game at all stages.

While introducing the beginner to the rules and moves of the game, *Teach Yourself Chess* also encourages the reader to think like a chess player, to perceive and formulate tactical ideas and strategy for himself.

Carefully graduated so as to demonstrate all stages of the game, and complete with illustrations, this lucid study of chess provides a valuable guide both for the novice and for the advanced player.

TEACH YOURSELF BOOKS

CARD GAMES FOR THREE

DAVID PARLETT

Playing cards is an entertaining and absorbing way to pass any evening and this collection of 3-hand games is ideal for the family as well as for serious card players who lack a fourth for Bridge.

This section includes the best 3-hand card games from all round the world; Pinochle from America, Skat from Germany, Five Hundred from Australia, Zwikken from Holland, Tyzicha from Russia, Calabrasella from Italy, Ombre from Spain. In every case the rules and questions of strategy are illustrated by sample games.

This is a book for both beginners and experts. The basic principles of card play are explained and some of the games are elementary, but several rival even Bridge in depth.

TEACH YOURSELF BOOKS

CARD GAMES FOR FOUR

DAVID PARLETT

Here is a selection of four-hand games which will cater for all tastes. There are two-against-two partnership games such as Whist, one-against-three games, such as Solo, and all-against-all (cut-throat) games such as Rummy.

The rules and procedure of every game are carefully and fully explained and sample games are included to illustrate play and demonstrate tactics.

David Parlett is a recognised authority on card games and the author of CARD GAMES FOR THREE.

TEACH YOURSELF BOOKS